# From Credit
# Crunch to
# Pure Prosperity

First published by O Books, 2010
O Books is an imprint of John Hunt Publishing Ltd., The Bothy, Deershot Lodge, Park Lane, Ropley,
Hants, SO24 0BE, UK
office1@o-books.net
www.o-books.net

| Distribution in: | South Africa |
|---|---|
| | Stephan Phillips (pty) Ltd |
| UK and Europe | Email: orders@stephanphillips.com |
| Orca Book Services | Tel: 27 21 4489839 Telefax: 27 21 4479879 |
| orders@orcabookservices.co.uk | |
| Tel: 01202 665432 Fax: 01202 666219 | Text copyright Maggy Whitehouse 2009 |
| Int. code (44) | |
| | Design: Stuart Davies |
| USA and Canada | |
| NBN | ISBN: 978 1 84694 328 7 |
| custserv@nbnbooks.com | |
| Tel: 1 800 462 6420 Fax: 1 800 338 4550 | All rights reserved. Except for brief quotations |
| | in critical articles or reviews, no part of this |
| Australia and New Zealand | book may be reproduced in any manner without |
| Brumby Books | prior written permission from the publishers. |
| sales@brumbybooks.com.au | |
| Tel: 61 3 9761 5535 Fax: 61 3 9761 7095 | The rights of Maggy Whitehouse as author have |
| | been asserted in accordance with the |
| Far East (offices in Singapore, Thailand, | Copyright, Designs and Patents Act 1988. |
| Hong Kong, Taiwan) | |
| Pansing Distribution Pte Ltd | |
| kemal@pansing.com | A CIP catalogue record for this book is available |
| Tel: 65 6319 9939 Fax: 65 6462 5761 | from the British Library. |

Printed by Digital Book Print

# From Credit Crunch to Pure Prosperity

Maggy Whitehouse

BOOKS

Winchester, UK
Washington, USA

# CONTENTS

# Chapter One

# The Credit Crunch and the Law
# of Attraction

*"The only thing we have to fear is fear itself – nameless, unreasoning, unjustified terror which paralyzes needed efforts to convert retreat into advance."*

Franklin D. Roosevelt said these immortal words in 1933 at the time of the Great Depression.

How right he was. Whenever we are told repeatedly that there is a problem, particularly a problem with something that carries as much emotional weight as money, we are bound to feel afraid. It is the human ego's natural response to negative outside stimuli. But in the modern world, fear itself is the root of most of our problems. Fear – or adrenalin – was designed to make us either run away or to attack. Both of these are appropriate reactions if we are faced with an angry grizzly bear. Both are totally inappropriate if we are dealing with intangible matters such as love, happiness – and money.

Money is intangible? Yes indeed. Money only exists in the mind of humanity. It is less "real" today than it ever has been. When we first invented money it was a token of something tangible such as a sheep or a precious metal. Nowadays, mythical amounts of energy pass between bank accounts with the validation of a piece of plastic. Mathematics keeps a score but nothing of true value actually changes hands any more. The value is all in our minds.

A financial expert on BBC radio who was discussing the beginning of the credit situation said, "It turns out that all this prosperity we've been experiencing is only based on imaginary money!"

He sounded really angry. But if the money was imaginary in the first place, then the problems with the money must also be imaginary. And the imaginary money is still there. If it's all imagination, then it's up to us to choose what we want to imagine.

Can it really be that simple? Yes it can. But simple isn't the same as easy.

First we need to work out why we got to think that it was complicated.

Thanks to the DVD of *The Secret*, the teachings of Abraham-Hicks and many other best-selling authors and spiritual mentors, the idea of the Law of Attraction has become widely known. It works on the simple principle of "like attracts like" or "birds of a feather flock together."

The idea of the Law of Attraction may only recently have become mainstream but it is not a new discovery. It is at the heart of the Hindu principle of karma (what you put out comes back; what goes around comes around) and it is evident throughout great religious texts including the Bible. Deuteronomy chapter 30 verse 19 puts it quite succinctly: "I call Heaven and Earth to record this day on your account, that I have set before you life and death, blessings and curses; therefore choose life, so that you and your seed may live." (KJV)

Judaeo-Christian mystics have always taught what we would now call the Law of Attraction as a way of understanding how life works and how to lead a happy and prosperous life; they just didn't call it by the modern name.

The Law of Attraction is immutable. It means that we attract into our lives the things that we resonate with.

All of life is vibration and what you think and feel dictates the level of your personal vibration. When we feel good, we have a high vibration and when we feel bad, we have a low vibration.

It follows that if thinking about a new home, a good job or a wonderful relationship makes us feel good, then we need to maintain that level of vibration to attract what we want. Lowering our vibration with thoughts of lack puts us out of alignment with anything that could bring us joy, and therefore it cannot show up in our experience.

Those of us who focus on love, prosperity and happiness attract exactly what we are thinking about – and those of us who worry, fret and beat ourselves up attract more reasons to become upset or dissatisfied.

## But how can I be attracting it if I don't want it?

The Universe, the Source, the Chi, the Creative Force, God, whatever you want to call it does not recognize the word "not" as in "I do *not* want this." When we say, "I do not want to be broke," It only hears the emphasis on the idea of being *broke*.

You can test this out for yourself by thinking of how much you don't want to be in financial trouble or something else that you don't want that would upset you. If you observe your thoughts, you'll see that if you dwell on the not wanting of a subject for just one minute, more negative and unhappy thoughts start to seep into your mind about the likelihood of exactly what you don't want coming to pass. You get to feel worse and worse and your vibrational level drops.

The same goes for happy thoughts too. Think happy things and more happy thoughts come. But for reasons that we will examine in this book, in the modern world, thoughts of prosperity seem to be harder for we humans to access. Certainly they are harder to find when there is already a negative thought entwined within our mind.

Since the advent of New Thought Churches such as *Unity*, founded by Charles and Myrtle Fillmore in 1889, and the world-famous *The Power of Positive Thinking* by Norman Vincent Peale, first published in 1952, the idea of affirming a positive thought to create a better situation has become a basic principle for those interested in creating a better life for themselves. To affirm good for one's self, such as saying, "I am healthy, wealthy and wise," is intended to re-program the mind instead of letting it habitually focus on negativity, which leads to a low vibration.

Affirmations work to a certain extent. They work when they do not oppose any deep inner belief or when the desire to change our life is so powerful that we feel it in the core of our being.

When my first husband died and my media career as an expert on China hit the impasse that was Tiananmen Square in 1989, I was desperate enough to engage in the idea of positive thinking for the first time. I tried affirmations and found that they brought great relief. I was in such pain that I was desperately seeking anything that would help, so I threw myself into the work of changing my thoughts.

However, once I began feeling a little better, the impulse faded away as my internal opposition set in. I began to think that I probably shouldn't be too happy as it would be disrespectful to Henry's memory; it would look as though I wasn't grieving, and I believed that I had to grieve if people were to believe that I had loved him. It would just be preposterous to appear be happy when I was a young widow or when my whole career had gone down the pan. People would think I was crazy.

I didn't have such resistance to the idea of earning a living – after all, my ego thought, if I was miserable enough I was bound to earn money wasn't I?

It's this kind of inner programming which is at the root of our habitual negative thinking and which can so easily scupper our efforts to make our lives better. It is known as *resistance* and it is very powerful. Resistance must never be underestimated or discounted. That way it gets to win. And if it wins, we remain unhappy and broke.

In my case, my unhappiness was such that my subconscious mind felt the situation to be verging on a threat to my survival. If I died, my subconscious would die too. Therefore, it did not put up resistance to something that would rekindle the desire to go on living within me. Once that had been achieved, any more was unnecessary and could make me a target for the derision or even hatred of others. That's the point where resistance kicked in.

Here's an example of how our mind works:

"I want to be prosperous and happy."

'I don't have enough money; I don't have enough money. I didn't have enough money when they said everything was economically sound. I'm going to have even less now there's a crisis. What I have got will be taken away.'

"I want to be prosperous and happy."

'I want doesn't get ... I can't ask to be prosperous when there are people in trouble. Other people would hate me.' Or 'It's not fair; I never get what I want. I hate money. Why does it always have to be about money? I'm a good person. I do my best. No one appreciates me. I'll probably lose my job in this credit crunch. It's not fair.'

"I want to be prosperous and happy."

'But I don't have enough money; you don't have enough money. It says so in the paper. It says so on the news. We don't have enough money. I don't like not having enough money. You don't like not having enough money. I must listen to the people on the radio who are complaining about *them* so I won't feel alone in this. So I won't have to blame myself. It's always *them*. It's *their fault*. *They* did this to me. *They* did this to us. We must shout against *them* and make *them* change things so that it's better for us. There's nothing I can do for me but I can shout about *them*.'

By the Law of Attraction we have put out three positive desires of wanting happiness and *more than thirty* negative desires about lack.

Don't doubt for one minute that the Law of Attraction will respond to that ratio. It's not a conscious force that thinks: "They don't really mean all that complaining; all they mean is the good stuff." It can't do that. All it can do is give us an exact mirror of what we think and feel and with that ratio of negative to positive thoughts, our vibration cannot be at the level of prosperity.

The so-called credit crunch (I won't give it capitals because that gives it a proper name and names are very powerful to the human psyche) came about through just such a process. We created it through toxic thinking.

## Toxic Fashion

For years, the world's economy has been expanding, with more building, more services, more goods to be purchased. Marketing (the modern-day magic) has thrived through teaching us by repetition that we *must have* this product or that concept. For example, people in the Western world have spent millions of pounds taking up carpets and laying wooden or laminate floors because they were told that those were the fashionable floors to have. Both kinds of floors work; it's just marketing that has swayed us. In the same way, we have all recently changed the design of our spectacles to suit the fashion where the previous style worked perfectly well. Fashion creates desire within a tribal society that wants to be seen to be up with the pack leaders.

But in the four or five years before the economy did its downturn, people were starting to say, "This can't go on. Houses are too expensive. I can't afford to buy." "My job isn't paying enough for me to buy all the things that I want to buy. I will feel better if I have a Louis Vuitton bag, but I can't afford one. Oh, never mind, I'll get it on a credit card. Now I can't pay my credit card off. It's not fair. Look at all those wealthy celebrities. They can afford Louis Vuitton and I can't. I can't pay my bills; I don't have enough money to keep up. I must keep up. My friends all have designer handbags so I need my Louis Vuitton. In fact, I need a Chanel bag now because Felicity has three designer bags. I can't afford it; it's too much."

And at the same time, the politicians and the economists have been saying, "The bubble has to burst; it's all going to end in tears; the expansion's too much" and journalists have been looking (as journalists do) for sensational news stories that dwell on the negative.

In 1993, a British newscaster, Martyn Lewis launched a "good news" campaign suggesting that the constant diet of crime and catastrophe that the news feeds us was unhealthy and should be counterbalanced by positive stories with happy outcomes. The press – and much of the public – heaped scorn upon him and Lewis lost a lot of work. The simple truth is that good news is no news because our egos are more comfortable with latching onto the drama of bad news.

Nowadays, with extraordinary levels of complaint, criticism and toxic gossip skidding across the internet, and a culture of blame, we are harnessing the Law of Attraction magnificently. The trouble is that we are activating it in a way that cannot help us to thrive.

Luckily, the natural state of this Universe is abundant; it is predicated towards good. It that were not the case, we would have imploded with the advent of television soap operas. But enough is enough.

## How We Create "Truth"

We create everything in our own lives and the irony is that we create nearly all of it by default; simply by reading or listening to the views of others and believing them.

Strangely enough, it is belief that creates truth, not the other way around. So if a number of people believe something, it becomes a truth. Enough people locked into the idea that there was a financial problem to make it come into being. But the good news is that *it doesn't have to be that way*. Each one of us can create or resolve a financial issue completely on our own. Yes, of course, it's easier if everyone else goes along with us. but prosperity is a very personal thing. As long as you can raise your vibrationary level and work at the level of the Soul, not the Ego, then the outside world's affairs don't have to affect you at all. Then, if you prosper, you can teach others how to do it too.

At the moment, I am more prosperous than I have ever been, despite what would seem to be an outside problem. But I have had two great credit crunches of my own in the past, one of which was in line with the outside world's thinking (the dot-com crash) and the other which was entirely personal.

In fact I've personally used the knowledge and techniques in this book to bring me back to prosperity from widowhood, divorce, business crashes, a failed emigration attempt, loss of several homes, career and the beliefs that I was stupid, inadequate and unworthy of love, happiness and money.

I'm still learning – this is a life's work. But hopefully, by using this book as one of your guides in creating a happier life, you can take a few more short-cuts than I did.

You don't have to be affected by the outside world; it is all about you. *Your* choices, *your* energy, and what *your* vibration is attracting.

Indecision and not choosing is just as much a choice making a conscious decision. Those who don't choose, rise or fall with the state of the world because they are working from the Ego state. Those who do choose are coming from the level of the Soul. It is the Soul which has the ability to step up and over everyday conditions. But in the secular world, we barely know, let alone understand the difference between Ego and Soul.

If you're not comfortable with the idea of Soul – the immortal aspect of each of us – you can substitute the idea of consciousness or Self. What is important is not the terminology but the ability to think and act consciously. It is perfectly possible to live a prosperous and comfortable life no matter what the outside circumstances might be. And that is not a selfish thing to do. Those who prosper inspire others and by learning how to live an abundant life you can teach others to do the same.

After all, no one will ever come up to you and say, "Do tell me, please – what is the secret of your failure?"

Chapter Two

# The Nature of Ego

Before we focus on the Soul, we need to identify the Ego. Like the Soul there are many other words for it such as sub-conscious, the inner child, the reptilian brain or the tribal level of consciousness.

Some spiritual beliefs believe that the Ego is bad and must be dissolved. I prefer the view that, like fire, it is a good servant but a bad master. We need the Ego for everyday life but we do not need it to dictate *how* we live.

Scientifically, the Ego is a part of the brain called the reticular activating system and it is a survival mechanism which works perfectly in a tribal situation but not quite as well in the modern, civilized world.

Everything we see, hear and experience is filtered through this reticular activating system of the brain so as soon as we believe something, we see more and more evidence of "the truth."

When we live at the level of the Ego state (and most of us live there for 90 per cent of our lives) then we are directly influenced by the news, the views of family, friends, teachers and peers. If they are reporting or anticipating a problem, especially with images which are a very powerful programming tool, then pretty soon, we'll start imaging – or imagining – it too. And in imagining it, we will believe it. And in believing it we will manifest it in our lives.

The reticular activating system filters literally millions of bytes of information every second. Without it, we would go mad.

Imagine if you were trying to concentrate on this book but your eyes were seeing everything else in the room, above, below, in front and either side of you with exactly the same level focus as the words in front of your eyes.

Imagine that, at the same time, every external sound was registering clearly in your consciousness with equal intensity.

Imagine that you were, simultaneously, aware of every cell in your body sending messages to your brain, reporting on its state of being.

Imagine being totally conscious of the air on every part of your body that is exposed and the material of your clothes everywhere else.

If I now say "your left foot" you are immediately conscious of that foot and that all is well with it. But thirty seconds ago, the messages sent from that foot were outside of your consciousness and, although the foot would obey your every command, it was totally taken for granted, not something you were acutely conscious of. Its messages were filtered out of your immediate awareness because you didn't need to experience them.

The reticular activating system decides, through training, what you need to know and what you don't need to focus your attention on right now, so that you don't go crazy with all the signals your brain receives. It is incredibly useful. Every signal comes in through the five senses and is passed on to your consciousness *only* if knowing about it is necessary.

If a brick falls on your left foot, the signal to the reticular activating system changes and it informs you immediately.

But how does it learn what messages it is necessary to pass on to the consciousness and which should be on "mute"? The system learns through repetition. It is programmed to ensure our survival. Without it we wouldn't remember how to co-ordinate our arms and legs so as to get out of bed in the morning. We wouldn't be able to stumble down the stairs and prepare our breakfast without giving it a second thought while listening to whatever the radio or TV instructs us should be our load of external information for the day.

In the days of our ancestors, the reticular activating system learnt swiftly to obey our elders who had essential survival knowledge and who could teach us which predators there were and how to avoid them; what plants could be eaten and which were poisonous; the uses and dangers of fire and water; how to build a shelter and how to recognize friend and foe. It was vital and useful and generally, benign.

It also programmed our psychological behaviour. Any human child needs more than just food. It also needs attention, preferably love. Only with that will it learn enough to survive within the social structure of our complicated species. So it will learn what behaviour is appropriate to get that love. Even today we still see images of children suffering from neglect in orphanages who have not got fully developed Egos. Food is not enough; without sufficient attention, a human child cannot grow into a balanced adult. If there is too little stimulus for basic survival skills, the child will simply die.

Your reticular activating system watched and learnt from your parents, teachers and peers from the day you were born. It assessed what worked and what didn't from the basics of "fire burns" and "look both ways before crossing the road" to "if I do that, Mum gets cross", and by absorbing the feelings and the sayings of all the people around you. In the case of emotionally absent parents, it will do all it can to gain their attention, including becoming a rebel or a difficult child.

The Ego will learn all it needs to know about appropriate psychological behaviour by the age of seven. This is all well and good if the messages it has received from parents, peers, teachers, are constructive and complementary – but frequently they are not. It is also well and good if they are open-minded in a world where all different beliefs, races and cultures live together. But overly tribal belief systems nowadays are often actively harmful.

The Jesuits have a saying: "Give me the child until he is seven and I will give you the man", meaning that a child's belief system will be formed forever in his or her first seven years. When it comes to beliefs about religion, money, social status and "right and wrong" that is absolutely so. It takes a conscious decision to change a belief after that time; perhaps a life-changing event such as the death of a spouse or a catastrophic accident.

If your parents often said "it's a lousy day" or "I hate the office" or "it's all right for some" or "money doesn't grow on trees" – just as idle words – those words got stored in your mind and were judged as appropriate by the reticular activating system. It was the way your tribe spoke and believed so it was the necessary path to follow for conformity and therefore safety.

The Ego also looks for proof that what it has been taught is true; that is, it seeks out circumstances and people who will believe and say the same thing. Words that contradict these primary beliefs cannot be true and must be proven not to be true because they feel dangerous. That's the root cause of resistance – and of religion and war. And that's why some people get so angry when they are contradicted.

In fact, the reticular activating system is just like a computer. If you try to input new data and it doesn't have a folder where that data can fit, or its ram is completely full with previous programming, it will reject the data.

New data is only dealt with by the part of you which is awake – the conscious Self, which is the doorway to the Soul. This Soul is the real you and the reason that you feel so alive when something unusual or different is happening is because you've been catapulted out of the everyday Ego Mind into the Self and the Soul. No matter how dreadful war may be, you will find that people who experienced it say they had never felt so alive as when they were a part of war, because they were experiencing something new every day. Any life-or-death situation is the same. Release from the Ego into the Self is the reason why people climb mountains, bungee-jump, compete in sports, drive fast cars or ride horses. They have to be conscious in order to anticipate the dangers which could be totally unexpected.

Where the Ego uses past information to operate, the Self is

experiencing the now. Working together they are a very powerful team. The Ego knows how to ride the horse and how to balance when there is movement. But only the Self is alert to what is happening right now and what is coming up.

Once something has happened, it can be stored away for recall by the reticular system at any time. That's its job. It can't cope with anything first time around.

Do you remember learning to drive? The first lesson was exhausting as you had to focus on steering wheel, placement of feet, gears, looking all around you and listening to and obeying your teacher's instructions.

This is the Self and the Soul working in full consciousness. The Ego plays no part because it is a new experience. By the time you had passed your test, you had driven so many times that you knew what to do and the Ego could help out. But even so, the first time of driving on your own was new and different and you were totally alert again. I often ask people to remember the first time they took a car out on their own, whether they listened to the radio, talked on their Bluetooth or played a CD. "Good grief, no!" is the answer. They remembered praying that they would remember everything and that they wouldn't crash. For that drive, they were totally conscious.

However, a few weeks later, they set out for a friend's house in the car, listened to the radio or talked with a passenger and, when they reached their destination, they had absolutely no idea how they got there. That was the point where the reticular activating system took over, leaving the Self to deal with any new stuff.

If there is an accident or a crisis, the Ego hands back power to the consciousness and, as our level awareness affects our conception of time passing, that is one of the reasons why time slows down. The consciousness then takes charge, living totally in the now as opposed to using old information.

## Achieving the Impossible

There is a legendary story told by Jack Canfield, co-author of the *Chicken Soup for the Soul* series, of an old lady who managed to lift up a car when her grandson became trapped underneath it. This was plainly impossible but she just went ahead and did it.

The lady declined to talk about the event for years but eventually, a colleague of Jack's tracked her down and she agreed to talk about it. She said that the reason she wasn't comfortable in discussing it was because if she could do such an amazing thing, it was uncomfortable to realize all the other things that she could have done and never did throughout her life.

*The Ego believes in limitations, rules, regulations and impossibility. Consciousness just gets on and does the impossible.*

Ten years ago I needed to get my beagle dog, Didcot, back to the UK from the USA without quarantine. Didi was too old and too spoilt to survive in a kennel for six months but in those days quarantine was the law. The Passports for Pets scheme was about to set up in nearly a year's time but it was only for European dogs. It wasn't possible to do what I wanted to do, so my Ego gave up. But my desire to get my dog home was so great that my conscious Self came up with an idea of taking Didi to Europe and registering her with a vet in Europe so that she could come into the UK as soon as the Passports for Pets scheme started up. No one else had thought of this idea although, in retrospect it seems completely obvious. However, once I had set my heart on this, the Ego came in with, "You can't stay in Europe for six months with your dog; you've got to go back to the UK and earn a living. You won't be able to find someone to look after your dog in Europe. Where will you take her? It's stupid to even consider it."

My husband at the time fully concurred with my Ego's view but because the desire to bring my dog home was so great, I overruled the doubts and "shoulds" and did the impossible. Didi was the first dog ever to come into the UK from America (via Spain) on the Passports for Pets scheme. Once I had stepped out of the Ego's rule, the way unfolded for me, people turned up out of the blue to help me, and doors that no one knew even existed opened right up. The British Ministry involved in the Passports for Pets scheme even thanked me for coming up with the idea as other Americans had been complaining that their dogs weren't valid for the scheme. Within a couple of months there were several places in Europe which would look after your dog for the six-to-eight months stay in Europe that was required to get them in to the UK from the USA.

## Recession, what recession?

If you're feeling broke or worried or fussed, the reticular activating system will seek for evidence that it is right to feel that way. Firstly, it will look for similar experiences within your memory to access the "It isn't fair; this always happens to me" part that can justify the feeling and then it will encourage you to talk to other people who feel the same way or at least who will sympathize with you so that you can feel comforted in your pain. This feels good, so it encourages the Ego to seek more and more validation of its cause for upset. But the more evidence it finds that something is wrong, the more it adds to the spiral of doubt and fear and more and more comfort will be required.

You can see this easily in the economic recession. The news (the word comes from North, East, West and South, not from anything actually being *new*) is parasitic, feeding on a breaking story and following it up to add more and more emotion around it. Even if something generally regarded as good happens, someone will be dug out of the woodwork to oppose it or to say that it can't last or that it's built on fake principles.

The thoughts of the Ego go round and round and round like a rodent on an exercise wheel. In fact I like to call the *R*eticular *A*c*T*ivating *S*ystem the Rats in our head. Rats are intelligent creatures and excellent parents. When they are kept in good conditions, they thrive, but if they are kept in dirt and without good food, they become pests – even carrying disease.

It is the same with the thoughts that we think over and over again. Deepak Chopra says that the 98% of the thoughts we think today are the thoughts we thought yesterday. And if thoughts create things, then we need to change the thoughts if we want the future to be different.

We live in a world where we are bombarded with negativity from the media and from each other. It's not the media's fault – they wouldn't do it if we didn't give it any attention.

From the moment we wake up until we go to bed, the radio presents us with hourly news, 99% of which is the same stories repeated all day about bad things happening to people.

The TV listings for this particular evening as I write (terrestrial channels only) are about the aftermaths of drink driving; threatened species and environment, drug dealing; murder; suicide; how bad our food is; abuse against women; how to deceive people through magic — and that's just the factual programmes. The fiction ones feature the usual combination of crime, soap operas revolving around misfortune, betrayal and hard luck stories, jealousy and avarice, and a smattering of gossip.

Once we are on the slippery slope of believing that something bad is happening then more and more evidence is sought to confirm it. We also start to use the outside situation to blame others for whatever situation we might find ourselves in. "It's all the fat cats' fault; it's the government's fault; it's the education system's fault; it's the immigrants' fault; it's the non-believers' fault; it's *their* fault."

Believing in the negative is our tribal habit now, and in addition to a regular diet of bad news, it is fuelled by soap operas and TV series filled with anger, grief, death, blame, crime and violence.

We say they don't harm us – but the Ego would say that, wouldn't it? The Ego is a complex beast made up from years and years of data with added experience that we call "truth." We know that it is truth because the more data we hear, the more we believe in it.

Remember how the reticular activating system filters the information that comes in through our senses? That includes our eyes and ears. We say "seeing is believing" but the opposite is true. If we believe it, we will see it. The Ego actually decides what to present to our consciousness from what our eyes see and our ears hear. So if we are stuck in poverty consciousness ("nothing goes right for me; I don't have enough money; there's nothing I can do; it's not fair; other people get breaks but I don't; the world is against me; no one understands me") then it is virtually impossible for the reticular activating system to alert the consciousness to any good opportunity that it might see. Those who have money issues, for example, will simply not see details of a free offer in a shop window. If they do see it, they will immediately discount it as a con. As there is so much offered nowadays which has strings attached, it's quite understandable for the Ego to act suspicious over anything that purports to be good.

## Quick Identification of Ego

Everyone's Ego is different and each one is overlaid by training but each one has a basic characteristic which is both its strength and weakness. For example, a naturally stubborn Ego will resist programming that it doesn't like but, on the other hand, once any programming is there, it will fight to the death to keep its opinion unchanged.

There is a useful way to assess the basic characteristics of a person's Ego-consciousness: astrology.

While many people deride astrology based on the sun sign charts in the media, this ancient tradition, when practiced carefully, is a clear indicator of tendencies within each individual.

The British Kabbalistic astrologer Peter Dickinson sums it up with the phrase, "Astrology is what happens when you don't use your free will."

In this ancient form of Jewish mysticism (an older version than that of the modern Kabbalah Centre) the Ego is equated with the placing of the Moon in a person's birth chart. The Self is the Sun sign and the Soul is made up from the placement of Sun, Mars and Jupiter. Astrology is seen as a person's blueprint – the basic principles with which they are equipped to deal with life.

As most of us spend 90% of our time coming from Ego consciousness, we are quite correct if we say that we are nothing like our Sun sign. That would be because we are nearly always presenting from our Moon sign.

So if you want to discover the basic characteristics of your Ego, look up your astrological chart on the Internet. Of course there is a lot more to you than just that but it is a handy indication of how you react to life.

The Sun signs are divided between four basic elements – Earth, Water, Air and Fire. People's basic make-up will be predicated on one of these elements. For example, here are the typical *immediate* Ego reactions of each element to the statement: "Your house is on fire. What do you do?"

Earth: Get a bucket of water and start putting it out.

Water: Panic. Fret about others.

Air: Find out if it's true and if so, how it started.

Fire: Organize.

Here's a brief outline of how the twelve different signs of the Zodiac manifest as both positive and negative Ego consciousness.

## Aries

Positive – Able to give others a much-needed prod. Enthusiastic.

Negative – Always keen to start project but never finishing them. Impatient with others, especially when they appear slow.

Ego-resistance phrase: *"It's got to be done now or it's not worth doing at all."*

## Taurus

Positive – Steady and reliable; trustworthy. Passionate.

Negative – Slow to get started. Stubborn. Greedy. Lazy. Pedantic.

Ego-resistance phrase: *"I'm right; you're wrong."* or *"There's no point so why bother?"*

## Gemini

Positive – Playful. Charming. Great conversationalist.

Negative – Deceitful. Changeable. Can't stick to one project or job.

Ego-resistance phrase: *"I never said that; I would never say that!"*

## Cancer

Positive – Caring, nurturing. Supportive.

Negative – Over-protective, controlling and manipulative. Over-focused on family. Crabby moods. Attacks as a form of defence. Guilt. Regret.

Ego-resistance phrase: *"If you really loved me, you would/wouldn't do that."*

## Leo

Positive – Wonderful support for leader; the power behind the throne.

Negative – Envious of others in power; arrogant and unyielding.

Ego-resistance phrase: *"It's not fair. I could do that better."*

## Virgo

Positive – Works hard, happy with detail and specifics.

Negative – Over-critical, picky and fussy. Obsessed with duty.

Obsessive with health.

Ego-resistance phrase: *"I haven't finished. I've got to do this properly or not at all."*

## Libra

Positive – Seeks fairness and beauty in all things

Negative – Indolent. Covers up nastiness with prettiness. Compromises principles for "good" outcome. Won't make decisions.

Ego-resistance phrase: *"You don't mind, do you? It's all lovely really."*

## Scorpio

Positive – Brave, strong. Able to cope with anything. This is the person you would want to accompany you into hell should you ever have to go.

Negative – Paranoid. Secretive. Self-destructive. Self-doubt. Filled with hatred and guilt.

Ego-resistance phrase: *"Everyone hates me. It's all my fault."*

## Sagittarius

Positive – Boundless enthusiasm and faith. Philosopher. Able to see the wider view.

Negative – Never seeing what needs to be done up close. Tactless. Faithless.

Ego-resistance phrase: *"Of course I can do it. I can do anything."*

## Capricorn

Positive – Trustworthy, loyal, fair and truthful.

Negative – Unadventurous. Dislikes change, sticks to habit. Follows the letter of the law.

Ego-resistance phrase: *"It wouldn't be right; I can't let people down."*

## Aquarius

Positive – Revolutionary. Innovative. Great ideas and lateral thinking

Negative – Unpredictable, expects others to follow his/her revolution and not their own. Ruthless.

Ego-resistance phrase: *"I'm not doing it unless I can do it my way."*

## Pisces

Positive – Loving, open, spiritual and free.

Negative – No boundaries, doormat. Gets his/her own way through passive non-resistance.

Ego-resistance phrase: *"I don't mind, we'll do whatever you want."*

# Chapter Three

# Re-programming the sub-conscious

## Soul, Self and Ego

**The Ego** is the tribal part of us which lives on past data and seeks more data to confirm its belief system. Its purpose is to keep us safe as a part of a tribe. An albino or a loose cannon in a herd is something which will attract unwanted attention from outside predators. The Ego believes that we must stay within the safe belief systems that we all hold and it deals with past experiences and future projections.

**The Self** is the individual person. No one else's Self is like you. You are unique on all levels and capable of clear observation of situations, both within and outside of yourself. The Self is the watcher. Have you ever observed yourself doing something as though you were a dispassionate outsider? That is the Self watching the Ego. The Self is consciousness and it deals with new situations. The Self focusses on the *now*.

**The Soul** is the Self's link to a higher consciousness. It is the eternal part of you which is the gateway to a greater universe. Both the Self and the Ego die but the Soul does not. Your Soul is part of something much greater than just one individual but the gateway to the Soul is through the Self so individuation is an important part of personal development. That means the ability to step out of the Ego and think independently.

The Jewish mystical tradition calls the Self *Tiferet* a Hebrew word that means both truth and beauty. It identifies the Soul with *Tiferet* and two other attributes: Judgement (discernment) and

Mercy (loving-kindness). So the Soul is a mixture of truth, discernment and loving-kindness.

The Ego does not contain any of those; it takes other people's opinions of truth rather than discerning its own with love. It does not *choose*, it reacts. That is the fundamental difference.

How often have you heard a newsreader say, "We'll be getting reaction from both sides?" Reaction is just that – re-action, going over old views.

Response, on the other hand, comes from the Soul. The root of the word is Latin from *re-* "back" and *spondere* "to pledge." So to respond to someone is to give them a token of honorable goodwill in return.

- Ego fits in with the tribe and dislikes change.
- Self develops the individual and seeks change where there is a desire to develop.
- Soul seeks perfection and embraces change because it knows that it cannot be harmed or die and therefore nothing new can be harmful to it.

- Ego judges according to social rules.
- Self sets its own agenda.
- Soul encompasses all.

- Ego relies on repetitive information which it sees as truth.
- Self finds its own path according to its desires. (restore)
- Soul encompasses the common good to raise the level of humanity. Otherwise you need to delete 'Ego relies on repetitive invo…as it doesn't make sense without the three.

The whole idea, according to centuries of mystical and holistic teachings is that we humans are happy when the Soul is the leader with the Self making conscious choices and the Ego serving and supporting the two higher levels.

What we have, most of the time nowadays, is the Ego ruling the Self through fear, doubt and conditioning, and the Soul doing what it can to alleviate our suffering.

The Ego is a tricky little thing and will often deceive us into thinking that it is in the role of the Soul – working for the good of all. It is actually quite easy to tell whether that is the case or not. If the person working for the good of all is healthy, happy and prosperous themselves, then they are working at the level of the Soul but, if they are unhappy, broke, unsatisfied, frustrated, resentful, full of blame or generally discontent, then the Ego is using good works as a form of resistance so as not to allow the Self to develop.

Harsh words? Yes indeed. But they are important because the help given to others at the level of the Ego is only every temporary shoring-up help. It is like the old saying:

*Give a man a fish and you feed him for a day.*
*Teach a man to fish and you feed him for life.*

Ego help doesn't free the other person; instead it keeps them dependent on others to survive. Soul gives soul-food to raise the level of consciousness.

## How to begin the reprogramming process

To successfully reprogram the Ego to abundance thinking you have be an Ego-Whisperer like a dog or horse whisperer. You can't just beat it into submission.

As its primary purpose is to keep you a safe member of the tribe, you have to teach it that what you want to do is to the benefit of the tribe as well as for you. If you are afraid that becoming prosperous will make you the butt of envy or criticism, your Ego will resist. But if you can appreciate that learning prosperity whatever the outside conditions is a gift that you can share with the whole world, then the Ego will be more willing to comply.

It is a question of baby steps. As all of life is vibration, jumping from a fear or lack vibration to a hugely abundant one is too big a leap for most Egos to take. Have you ever been to a seminar or workshop that was truly inspirational? You came home filled with excitement and delight and confident that the feeling and the ideas would remain with you. But somehow, in the next week – or maybe after just one day in the office, it all seemed remote and unrealistic or, at the very least, too hard to maintain. Or maybe you just forgot it...

That's because the rise in vibrational level within you at the workshop was too high for your Ego to be able to maintain comfortably. But don't despair, slowly and steadily may not be as attractive as giant leaps, but maintaining a steady rise in vibration is the technique that truly lasts.

The first thing to do is to remind yourself that you are a spiritual being. You are not a body that happens to have an Ego, a Self and a Soul. You are a Soul that happens to have a Self, an Ego and a Body.

You are eternal and you come from a world that has no worries about money, time, possessions or happiness. It is always abundant and happy at the Source.

Religious training may not have taught you that – and there is a whole chapter on religious resistance to prosperity later on – but some part of you *does* know that somehow you should be happier and more in tune with the glory of life and less run-around with its pressures.

Whether or not you believe in what we call "God" you wouldn't be reading this book if you didn't have some concept of a creative force that is the Source of all things. This Source is not just a distant being (the archetypal elderly man with a long beard) but an essence of life force. It creates continually; every moment of life is a miracle of creation.

Every religious teaching in the world says that we are the

children of the creative force. And as Its children we too are creators, whether we like it or not. There is nothing on Earth which was not a thought before it was formed into a physical thing. There is not an emotion that was not preceded by a thought. We create constantly simply by putting our attention on something. We cannot stop creating. And we create by default if we don't do it consciously. So focusing on any financial recession or negativity towards money simply creates more of it. And then our Ego is justified in saying, "I told you that it was true!"

## Introducing your Martian

Some people work with the idea of their Higher Self, others work with guardian angels or guides, and others work with Universal principles. I suggest starting off with the idea of a Martian standing at your shoulder at all times.

This is an easier idea to grasp, because if we do have a spiritual belief we tend to think that our angels or guides know what we truly want and can filter out all the rubbish that we throw in around it.

But they don't.

They are cosmic beings who work solely with vibrational levels. The energetic beings that organize the Universe (who are known to us as angels) have never been human, and our discarnate human guides have forgotten what it is like to schlep around 140 pounds all the time. When you die, you slough off the physical and psychological heaviness and it is hard to remember exactly what it was like. Remember a time when you were ill – flu or something similar – and you swore that when you were better you would remember every day how grateful you were to feel good? Then within a day or so of being better, you forgot completely? It's like that when you don't have a body any more.

So let's work with a Martian instead. It is easier to understand that as a foreign being with no idea whatsoever about your culture, background, beliefs, attitudes or desires. *All* it can observe is your thought vibrations with the assumption that, as you have the gift of choice, you would choose the things you want to give your attention to. *And so it gives you everything that you give your attention to.*

Why doesn't it discriminate and give you just what you want? Do *you* even know exactly what you want? How can it possibly tell from your everyday thoughts? The spiritual teacher Eckhart Tolle says that the only difference between most of us and the crazy people who mumble, shout and swear in the street is that we do all our mumbling, shouting and swearing silently.

Let's focus on the idea that the Universe gives to us whatever it is we give our attention to. Most people in difficult financial times give their attention to lack, bills and money worries. And if that's where we put our energy, then the Universe is simply going to offer us more of the same.

That Law of Attraction is immutable.

But where do we start to turn all this around? I find that the very best starting point is going back in time and using a technique that is more than 3000 years old. It has become much misunderstood over the last centuries but hopefully this book will help you to unravel many practical and effective spiritual techniques which have been misinterpreted over the years.

What is so very special about this one is that it helps the subconscious which may be locked into Christian beliefs about "good people" being poor (see chapter five). The idea of Christian virtue and poverty is very powerful in the Western World whether or not we are actually Christians. It is also presented as a Christian belief that we must put charity before ourselves. But in fact this is *not* what the Bible says.

By reinterpreting just one ancient teaching from the Bible you can kick-start your subconscious into turning the tide of financial prosperity. Most Egos will believe a Biblical teaching more than a new-fangled holistic one simply because of old training.

## The Truth about Tithing

Most people think that tithing is a Biblical command to give the first ten per cent of your earnings to charity. However, the system was invented to harness the Law of Attraction. It does address an order of giving when money comes in – but it is emphatic that this is in order to bless you and to bring prosperity back to you.

The word "tithe" means one tenth but in ancient days a tenth did not necessarily mean a tenth of all your income, because most people didn't have an income! They dealt in trade and as a general rule, a tenth was one whole thing – as in one whole chicken, one whole sheep, one fig, one cheese. In the modern world, it can mean one whole banknote or one whole coin. There's no need to fear that you will be asked to give more than you can afford. One penny or one cent is a good first step in tithing. You can build up to the more traditional ten per cent if you want to.

The order of tithing is simple:

1 Spiritual Tithe (Leviticus 27:30)
2 Celebration Tithe (Deuteronomy 12:6, 17-18; 14:22-27).
3 Charity Tithe, (Deuteronomy 14:28; 26:12) every third year *only*.

In the modern age, it means give
... towards Spiritual Inspiration
... for celebration/gifts for yourself and
... to everybody else – including paying the bills.
In this way, you show the Universe (and your Martian) your priorities.

You want firstly, inspiration (ideas and chances to make your life happier), secondly, fun and festivity, and thirdly, to be prosperous enough to pay your dues and help others.

How most people practice this form of tithing is to have a couple of attractive bags or boxes; one for the inspiration tithe and one for the celebration tithe. They place a little bit of money in the boxes *first*. That money can then be saved up to buy something special. The important thing is that it means you have taken power and are stating to the Universe that you want prosperity and not debt or fear.

In the age of the internet, you can have a couple of online savings accounts named "inspiration" and "celebration" and move £1/$1 (or more) into those accounts as soon as possible once money has come in. Then pay the bills.

Most people actually think that it's important to put charity or bill-paying first but if you do that, then the Universe puts other people before you too, and will continue to do so. Focus on bills and you will receive more bills. If you put inspiration first then you will find very swiftly that there is always money to give to others/pay the bills but if you give to others/pay the bills first then there's never enough left for you...

Although the Bible talks about the first ten per cent being given to the Temple priests, this was because they were meant to be the source of inspiration to the populace. The priests did not have time to work for a living or tend flocks as they looked after the people's religious needs. Nowadays, priests are paid wages, and they may not be your source of inspiration.

That is the key – what inspires you? What takes you closer to your own personal relationship with Divinity? Is it a book you'd like to buy? Is it a workshop you'd like to go to? Is it an inspirational teacher you'd like to hear? That's where to put your money, and your Martian will give you more opportunities to be inspired. It may take you a few weeks to save up for what you want, but the money is there, in the box or the savings account, telling the Universe clearly what your priorities are.

The celebration tithe was, originally, to travel to Jerusalem for the great festivals four times a year. You would all travel together as an extended family, or even as a village, and while in Jerusalem would eat, drink, make merry and arrange marriages.

But the Old Testament is very clear that if you *can't* get to Jerusalem you should spend the value of the tithe on a feast (including strong drink) so it's a clear message to have fun.

When I was stony broke I turned my life around with this system. At the time I could only afford to put 50p/$1 in each of the pots at a time but that did mean that I felt more abundant than if I didn't have any hope whatsoever of getting a book to help me, a treat for supper or even a bar of chocolate.

Nowadays, I often use part of my spiritual tithe to buy a great bunch of white lilies for my meditation room because just seeing them inspires me. It's entirely personal what inspires you. The festival tithe ensures, at the very least, that there is always a bottle of champagne and a pack of smoked salmon in the refrigerator.

Of course it's fine to use your spiritual tithe as a gift for others who inspire you, but if you want to be prosperous, you will only be inspired by people who are already prosperous themselves, so be sure you distinguish between giving from true inspiration and giving to support or help someone. Charity is the third tithe, not the first one.

The tithing system is incredibly powerful. It tells the Universe what is important in your life. And it truly does work with 50p/$1. Of course you can give more if you want and you *will* want to as your financial prosperity increases.

There is also a fourth tithe in the Old Testament – the Sabbatical tithe. Every seventh year the land was rested and all debts forgiven. The land lay fallow so that it could replenish itself, and the people lived from the grain stock from the previous six years. They could do that because they were using the Law of Attraction to ensure that there would be abundant grain.

The forgiveness of debts is a lovely idea too. No one took on a debt for more than seven years – and although they were expected to make every effort to repay it, if they could not, the amount was forgiven and forgotten as part of the seventh year.

Nowadays, some of the more prosperous countries are forgiving Third World Debt. That can only be a good thing, and it's evidence that this is primarily a good and abundant world, even if it takes us a little while to get round to the idea.

Incidentally, the third tithe, the charity tithe was only given every third year. That was because, due to the way people lived, it wasn't needed any more often than that. We could do with a world where that is the case right now.

# Chapter Four

# Fear of failure / Fear of success

It seems strange in our celebrity and media-led world that there should be such a thing as a fear of success hidden in the heart of so many of us. But fear of success is an even stronger form of resistance than fear of failure.

Failure is a good place to hide. It has the comforting companions of "It's not my fault; I did my best" and "If it weren't for him/her/them/the economy/the government, I would have succeeded." So an economic downturn is quite a comfortable place for people to hide. "I can't do it now because of the economy."

The Soul can do anything, any time, anywhere, but the Ego runs with the pack. It's worth mentioning that sometimes "the pack" will be the pack of rebels. Joining an holistic centre, becoming an eco warrior or a Buddhist, generally just means joining a more unorthodox pack. Certainly when I began to be interested in holistic health and thinking I did the equivalent of a (very) late adolescent rebellion along the lines of: "I'm going to be nice to people *differently* so there!" Whenever we do anything to make a point, we do it from Ego.

## Celebrity Culture

Even before the lives and loves of the famous were paraded before us in magazines and on the internet, from our earliest youth we have been trained how to think. Usually, we were taught to put others first; to do what our mothers, fathers, teachers and peers wanted us to do.

The trouble is: they all wanted us to do, or be, something different. And doing what pleased one of them may have displeased another. No wonder we are confused. So it is easier to do nothing much at all.

It's less so in the USA but in Europe, we have what is known as "tall poppy syndrome" where a flower that grows taller than the others in the field risks being cut down because it doesn't fit in with the rest. That cutting down can be seen in the way magazines and entertainment shows focus on what's allegedly wrong in a celebrity's life from their relationship to their cellulite. In a world that worships youth and beauty it would be hard for any woman to have her flabby upper arms or under-eye bags plastered across the media or for any man to have his bald spot or his beer belly paraded for people to deride.

It may be for that reason that reality TV is so popular. Instead of the particularly talented or brilliant being the ones who are the most famous, it is the amateurs who are prepared to show off their personalities rather than their attributes. That way, we can all hope for Andy Warhol's famous "15 minutes of fame" without undue criticism. Even so, the folk who do stand out in the shows are chased and paraded and mocked. So the search for celebrity is, nowadays, just as much an Ego-calling to be insulted in public in order to prove our lack of worth as it is a search for the admiration of others.

Ouch.

There is also no possibility in real life of actually looking like the computer-enhanced, air-brushed images of Botoxed, face-lifted, hair extensioned, professionally made-up beauties (of both sexes) that we see in the media. Or if we do, then our lives must be devoted to physical enhancement and very little else which, to the Soul, is deeply unfulfilling.

Happily, development of the Soul leads to an inner beauty so that, no matter how much of a wattle you may be developing or whether your tummy has seen more slender days, there is a light within that still makes you beautiful to any observer (and more importantly to yourself).

Fear of failure and fear of success both keep us paralyzed in the safest position we can find. To try and to fail is to invite derision from others (this is the case in the UK though perhaps not as much in the success driven USA) and possibly even "I told you so" but at least you can justify to yourself and to others that you tried.

Yoda in *Star Wars* has it right: "There is do and there is not do. There is no *try*."

Having "tried and failed" quite dramatically in several areas in my life – including a marriage, an emigration, and running a company, I have avoided success in many different ways. I didn't for one moment think that I wanted to fail – consciously I didn't. But it was going to stick my head firmly above the parapet if I did succeed and the Rats in my head believed that was a dangerous thing to do.

## Subconscious Resistance
Here's how subtle this resistance can be:

The last couple of times we moved house we had the new place Feng Shui-ed by an expert. Feng Shui, like astrology, operates in the psychological world. In Jewish mysticism this is known as the world of forms, emotions or illusions. It can be overcome by free will – where you make a conscious decision and act on it. But if you don't use free will, then the world of forms will operate according to its innate energetic tendencies. It will work from its default position.

This is the same as the human Ego. Our subconscious will do all sorts of things that we, consciously, don't know about or even approve of, simply because of old conditioning. The "Chi" of land is basically old conditioning from the way the world turns and the landscape was formed. You can raise the "Chi" in a house by light, sound, images, invocation and scent, but unless you make significant changes or unless you keep raising it consciously, it will revert to its normal energy level. And one of the reasons that you will be attracted to that house is because its energy level reflects and resonates with yours.

The most significant change that our Feng Shui practitioner told me to make was to move my work desk. Obviously, not knowing the Feng Shui of the house, I hadn't intended to put my desk in a place which signified bad energy in fame/reputation. But I did. And as she pointed out, I had done that *in two houses running*. So why would I, subconsciously, put my desk in a place where the natural energy of the house would try and thwart my building a good reputation in my work? Do I want that consciously? Heck, no!

However, what I also had was a childhood memory of being told not to try and outshine other people; not to show off; not to demonstrate that women can be successful (for fear of showing up my very talented but then agoraphobic mother). And an adult injunction not to stick my head above the parapet (that one came from my spiritual teacher no less!).

So the "safety stand-by" or default position in my psyche has been "don't make yourself too visible" – and that's where it was going to stay unless I made conscious efforts to change it.

Further evidence of this within my own Ego? I had my first book published and made a TV documentary on China in 1988 and then married a man who became sick with terminal cancer within months. Bless him, my life changed for the better because of his love and presence in my life but the situation also gave me a great excuse for failing in a promising career by choosing to focus all my attention on Henry's health rather than applying a little balance and developing my career. By the time my husband died, the world-famous Beijing revolt in Tiananmen Square had happened and China was strictly off-limits for books, TV and documentaries. And I had no other career up my sleeve...

Ten years later, at the time when my first novel was published, my second husband and I decided to emigrate to Montana, USA, effectively removing me from all promotional activities for the book and taking me away from my publisher, the magazine I ran and a whole career that I had built in England. I chose to go – no blame is implied here. It was all me. The second book in the trilogy, which had been accepted and praised by my publisher, then failed to make it into print.

Oh come on, you may be saying. These are all external events. They can't just be you scuppering your career subconsciously! Believe me, they can.

What have you done to scupper yours?

That I've done well, and become happy and prosperous despite this earlier inner default position, is due to learning and teaching onwards the prosperity work that is now becoming ingrained in my psyche and operating on default. That's how to use the Rats in our heads for good. The deeper our knowledge of the Law of Attraction, the more we will understand that *there is always enough for everyone.* You don't create less for you by teaching others how to prosper; rather the reverse is the case. By re-training our Egos into prosperity consciousness we can relax, understanding that the flow of abundance is constant. But even so, it is still important to seek out the remaining unconscious scuppering techniques because they can be tricky little devils.

## Checking out your own resistance

So, do you have to have your house Feng Shui-ed to overcome fear of success so that you can be prosperous and follow your life's path? No. But it would help if you did the following:

## Check out your childhood conditioning about success.

What did your parents believe? Did they criticize other people who were a success? Did they say phrases such as "I would have been successful if so-and-so hadn't happened?" Do you think it might hurt them if you succeeded where they failed? Would they resent you or think you had it easy when they had it hard? Were they "top dog" and very successful themselves and you felt that you couldn't attempt to outshine them? Did you succeed in something and they criticized or mocked you for some aspect of your success?

And if they did want you to succeed – and even push you to succeed – and you haven't done so, is it possible that, subconsciously, you are punishing them by making sure you fail, just as a way to show them that they are failures as parents? That's just as big a block to prosperity as obeying parents who didn't want you to succeed.

## Move the furniture around and clear out the clutter in your home

"Chi" energy needs to flow around rooms; it gets blocked if there is no way that it can go. Try to arrange your home so that it is not full of objects that energy can't get past. Imagine that energy flows in circles around the edge of each room. Is there something obvious that would stop it dead?

Clutter clearing became very popular on TV over the last ten years but it has tended to focus on physical clutter. What emotional clutter do you have? Old angers, hatreds and resentments are also energy blocks to prosperity.

### Bless and cleanse your house

Do a home blessing ceremony as often as you can using flower remedies, holy water, aromatherapy oils, smudge sticks, Tibetan singing bowls, drumming, candles or whatever appeals to you. Such a conscious action over-rules the natural default energy of your home. If you did that every week then you would never need to have the house Feng Shui-ed and you'd never have a problem with energy flow because you would consciously be creating good energy on a regular basis.

### Check the pictures on your walls.

Your life is created by whatever it is you put your attention on. If you want love in your life, then have pictures on your walls depicting couples in love. If you want wealth, have images of lovely, beautiful things. Never, ever, ever, have pictures on your walls that depict poverty, grief or pain.

When I was a young, single woman I had pictures everywhere of young, brave, single, lonely women. I had to spend six weeks in China, totally away from my home, in order to reprogram my Ego enough to recognize a man who could commit to me. And believe it or not, the picture hanging over my bed was John Byam Shaw's "The Boer War" which depicted a sad young widow – which is what I was to become within a year of my marriage.

## Watch your idle words; they are creators.

If are in the habit of saying you are "sick and tired" of something or you are "fed up" with something, guess what you'll get. A friend once knew a man who was enjoying a holiday away from his work stresses so much that he said, repeatedly, "For two pins I'd stay here for a month." After the next day's skiing accident, he had two pins in his right leg and was in hospital for a month.

And never, ever refer to any credit crunch (let alone giving it capital letters!). Every mention of it as being real or difficult strengthens the belief in it.

## Don't hide your light under a bushel.

It is always worth considering the wonderful words written by Marianne Williamson and quoted by Nelson Mandela at his presidential inaugural speech in South Africa:

*"Our deepest fear is not that we are inadequate. Our deepest fear is that we are powerful beyond measure. It is our light, not our darkness that most frightens us. We ask ourselves, Who am I to be brilliant, gorgeous, talented, fabulous? Actually, who are you not to be? You are a child of God. Your playing small does not serve the world. There is nothing enlightened about shrinking so that other*

*people won't feel insecure around you. We are all meant to shine, as children do. We were born to make manifest the glory of God that is within us. It's not just in some of us; it's in everyone. And as we let our own light shine, we unconsciously give other people permission to do the same. As we are liberated from our own fear, our presence automatically liberates others."*

From *A Return to Love,* by Marianne Williamson *(Harper Collins)*

The whole purpose of prosperity work is about choosing happiness. Although we all want more money, usually the truth is that we want the experiences that we believe more money can bring us rather than just the money itself sitting and doing nothing in the bank. We want the lovely home; the relaxed lifestyle; the wonderful holidays, and the ability to say "yes please" to things we want to purchase whenever we want them.

It *is* lovely to have the cash in the bank but it's experiences that enrich us. And if we feel rich in any other way, the cash will follow. It's Universal Law.

Love the road and the destination is a delight. Moan and fret about the road and the destination is poor or non-existent.

Two years ago I had lunch with a friend who was about to marry a millionaire and it was both lovely and sad that she confided in me that she was having a hard time coping with people's reactions to her good fortune. Lovely because she could talk to me about the delight of having her fiancé buy her a brand new state-of-the-art car as a gift and talk about the fabulous wedding they were planning and know that I would celebrate with her, and sad because she felt she needed to hide her prosperity from some other friends and family because she was afraid they would sneer at her or say things like, "well it's all right for *you...*"

Famous people get a lot of reaction from people because of who they are and what they've done and very often it's hard for them to make friends. Every now and then, they are pining for someone just to chat to them about the weather or the news. I got to date TV chef Keith Floyd for a while simply because he was staying overnight in Birmingham to do a show that I was a part of and I took him home and gave him baked beans on toast and a night in watching the telly. Most people cooked him elaborate meals and fussed over him in those days and it was a huge relief that someone treated him like a normal bloke.

Incidentally, the lady who's marrying the millionaire had done a lot of prosperity work – not to catch a millionaire but to create enough space in her life for a partner. She had been single for a very long time and until she realized that she had filled her life up to the point that there was no room for a lover and it was barren of potential mates. Once she cleared the space and started putting herself in places where she could meet people, it only took nine months for the love of her life to show up. Then, of course, we had to work with her resistances to love. She wanted him to look different; act differently; respond differently; but it was all resistance to her own good fortune. Once she gave in and allowed him into her life as a friend and then a lover, the transformation was complete.

I'm not surprised he's so wealthy; this friend has always selected the best. She cut corners when she felt broke but she always made sure that her hair was clean and her (very simple) make up was immaculate. She didn't buy many clothes but the ones she bought were classic and good quality. She looked like a millionaire, she walked like a millionaire and she believed in her own prosperity whatever the outside circumstances.

## From Lack to Abundance

Here's an example of turning lack consciousness (Ego) into prosperity consciousness (Soul):

Some years ago when my husband Lion and I were feeling less

prosperous than today, we went on a city break to Florence, Italy. We selected a lovely-looking restaurant for our last night there and I went in and ordered us a glass of red wine for us both while he found somewhere to park the car. The wine arrived – but you had to look for it! It was a medium-sized glass with less than a third of it filled with liquid. The intellectual part of me knew that this is the epicurian way of serving the best wines in Florence, where quality is appreciated beyond quantity and where in the very best enoteca wine cellars and restaurants, the glass is only filled about one third full in order to allow the wine to breathe and be savored at its best. But my Ego only saw lack. As I looked at it my glass seemed to be 'half empty', and as I thought about the price, I started getting resentful. Poverty consciousness was fervently pursuing the following thoughts: "It's not fair. I know we can't drink much because we are driving but this is ridiculous. I'm not paying another huge amount for a second glass of this. It's not worth the money. It's a rip-off. This is our last night and we've chosen the wrong restaurant. It's all ruined. I'm so angry. Who do they think they are? I'll have finished this before the food comes and then I won't enjoy my food..."

But then a little warning light went on in my head. I knew I had a choice to think thoughts that would hurt my own enjoyment or I could make the effort to think thoughts that would feel good.

If I carried on thinking I had been hard done by, it would only ruin the evening we had planned. If I recognized that this was a special treat, it would make it a lovely evening. It should have been a no-brainer really – our thoughts create our experiences, after all. It wasn't easy as I stared resentfully at the small measure of wine in my glass, but I gave it a go.

I decided to think about the fact that the wine was there, now, waiting to be drunk. It was silly to fuss about there not being any more to come as I hadn't tried what there was! Instead I decided to focus on admiring the beautiful color of the wine. It was a glorious garnet color and, as I looked at it I could see how beautiful it was and how the light glowed within it with different hues as I turned the glass around. I smelled it, as an expert would, and I let my senses soak in its scent. Each inhalation was different and without following it immediately with a drink, I could appreciate it differently. And I looked through the glass at the lovely restaurant noticing the distortions of the light that the glass caused and then I became so interested in the fact that it was obviously a hand-made glass presenting different views that I didn't even take a sip until Lion had arrived. He raised his glass and toasted us and we drank – and it was perfect.

I took great care to make that glass last until we had eaten and I treasured every sip.

And you know what's really amazing is that it's the only glass of wine I've ever drunk that has stayed completely in my memory. I can still see, smell and taste that one glass of wine in my mind six years later and it is that memory that comes into my Ego's thoughts every time anyone mentions red wine. Now that is value for money...

## Chapter Five

# The root of all fear about money

It's all too easy to blame whatever we believe in (especially the emotionally-loaded word *God)* and to suppose that something bigger than us doesn't want us to be rich. But the Source Energy didn't invent money, *we* did. It's one of humanity's most amazing creations. It's just a system of harnessing energy that was invented to make things fair so that people could swap products around without having to do a straight trade. I may have pigs and you have chickens and I want some of your eggs. But you don't want pork; you want lamb. So I give you a token in exchange for your eggs which you can give to the lamb farmer in return for one of his sheep. Then the lamb farmer comes to me, gives me back the token and has one of my pigs.

Even further, suppose that one year, my pig dies but I still need eggs from your chickens, so I offer a token to promise that next year I will give two haunches of pig instead of the usual one, as long as I can still have the eggs. That token is a promise of commitment and it will be honoured by me and, should I die, by my family.

What a sensible idea! That's it. That's all that money is; an agreement of trade between two people.

Our fear over money works in the same way that we fear God. I'm going to call the Source Energy God here because this is the problem that is the biggest we face in prosperity consciousness: the mythical all-powerful old man in the sky who judges us. Our Egos think that we'll get shouted at for letting the pig die in the first place and then, when we've continued having the eggs for an extra year, it resents giving the second haunch of pig. That's just Ego being silly and unfair. It has nothing to do with whatever we might call God.

If we fear this Source Energy and don't think we are worthy of Its love then we will also fear money for exactly the same reason, because money is energy just the way that life-force is energy. It is an energy onto which we project great power, so it isn't that different to our Ego from its perception of God.

Fear attracts exactly what is feared – if we focus on lack we will create it, but if we focus on prosperity we will create that instead.

## Religious Misinterpretation

But why did we get so confused? The majority of the Western World's Ego problems with money come from a deep belief that has been prevalent for nearly 2000 years. It pervades Christianity and, through centuries of misinterpretation where we believed that you had to be poor to be judged good, it has been the source of great poverty where it actually sought to enrich the soul. So many people know – and believe – the misquoted phrase, *money is the root of all evil.*

The full quotation from St. Paul's letter (1:10 Timothy) is: "Having food and raiment let us be therewith content. But they that would be rich fall into temptation and a snare, and many foolish and hurtful lusts, which drown men in destruction and perdition. For the love of money is a root of all evil: which while some coveted after, they have erred from the faith, and pierced themselves through with many sorrows."

The word translated as "love of money" is *philarguria* and it means avarice or greed, and Paul is trying to make it clear that *focussing* on financial wealth over all other things is harmful to the soul. To do so is to make money a god rather than a tool.

Paul does not say that money should be hated or despised – just that it should not be made the whole object of existence. People tend to think that "having food and raiment, let us therewith content" means that we should live with the minimum of comfort, but that is not its correct translation at all. It is vital to look at the Biblical meaning in the context of the time. Nobody in Paul's time had a mortgage nor gas and electricity bills – but if they had, the Greek word that is translated as "food" would cover all those. The word is *diatrophe* which means *a sufficient supply of that which nurtures and sustains us*. It's not just referring to enough to eat, but all that we need to sustain a pleasing and nourishing life. In the modern world that word could perfectly well include holidays, a good car, a decent audio-visual system and regular pay rises.

Often I ask people if they would worry about money if they knew that there would never be any mortgage, rent or tax to pay, no bills, if clothing came free for their children in the next size up to allow for the next year's growth, and if they knew that they would always have all that they needed to eat and to supply their home. The answer is always "no."

Paul says that "some" have erred from their faith through focussing on financial gain, not that *all* are prone to do so.

Incidentally, the word translated as "evil" is *kakos* from which we get the word kak meaning dung or shit … and *philarguria*, the word used for "love of money" also refers to obsession with money when you don't have any – the fuss and worry over whether we have enough.

So a perfectly valid and contemporary translation could read, "obsessing over money or the lack of it leads to a rubbish life." Anyone who's been broke knows that that is true enough.

## Was Jesus really poor?

Jewish and Islamic peoples, as a general rule, don't have the in-built belief that it is important for good people to be poor, in the same way that poverty is built into Christianity. The Patriarchs of the Torah all became wealthy men and the Prophet Mohammad was a prosperous merchant. However, living in nominal Christian countries, this prevalent belief can still rub off whatever your belief system and even if you don't have one at all.

Jesus was despised, rejected and poor, right? That's what we are told every Christmas. But there is no actual evidence in the Bible to show that Jesus of Nazareth lived a life of poverty. This assumption is simply misinterpretation of an ancient lifestyle.

Certainly, Jesus was not a fan of cluttering yourself up with possessions so that you were too tied down by responsibilities to be able to follow your heart and soul. But his life was a series of miracles of prosperity beginning with his birth and continuing through celebrations like the wedding at Cana, not to eclipse the miracle of his resurrection.

So how did we get it so wrong? Firstly, from centuries of teaching that poverty and spirituality were an appropriate match as demonstrated in an over-emphasis on New Testament sayings such as *"It is easier for a camel to go through the eye of a needle, than for a rich man to enter into the kingdom of God."* The Greek word for a "rich man" is *plousios* which means someone abundant in possessions and it is certainly true that it is harder to be centered in our authentic Self (the Jewish mystical interpretation of "kingdom of heaven") when we are filled with responsibilities and weighed down by possessions.

Back in the 16th century, the mystical Rabbi Isaac Luria told his followers that the Messiah had come and they should go with him to Jerusalem immediately. None of them would or could because of their homes, families, jobs. Luria said it as a test to see whether those who professed to want to meet the Messiah more than anything could live up to their word. They couldn't. And probably neither could most of us follow our heart's desire because of all the *stuff* in our lives. So do we possess our possessions or do they possess us?

One of the greatest weapons used by those wishing to attack the basis of Islam is the "proof" that Mohammed was not a holy man because of his wealth, his merchant and warrior status and the fact that he married a rich older woman – and had a total of

22 wives and concubines during his life.

In contrast, Jesus is held up as a paragon of virtue due to his life as an itinerant preacher with no possessions and his crucifixion. Buddha walked away from a life of riches; Ghandi lived in poverty; Mother Theresa lived with the poor in Calcutta, and we hear about saints such as St Francis and St Clare, who legend tells, lived lives of such self-denial that they became physically ill. Most saints from ancient times lived lives of self-sacrifice and self-mortification, offering horrific examples of what it means to be holy. We are told of virgins who mutilated themselves to avoid being found attractive or forced to marry; and at the very least, of men and women who threw off their robes of wealth, dressed in coarse cloth and shut themselves away from all society to devote their lives to prayer. The former includes St Rose of Lima who, from the age of 20, wore a metal spiked crown, concealed by roses, and an iron chain about her waist. She would fast for days, taking just a drink of bitter herbs and when she could no longer stand, she sought repose on a bed constructed by herself, of broken glass, stone, and thorns. That's not holy; it's a denial of God's goodness and of life itself. Today, Rose would be considered anorexic, self harming, psychologically damaged, and seriously in need of help.

If we believe that God demands such sacrifice of us in order to be good people, how can we possibly justify having enough cash to live a comfortable life?

We are also taught that Jesus was a carpenter and the implication is that this was not an impressive thing to be. But the Greek word translated as "carpenter" in the Gospels is *"tekton"* which actually meant artisan, mason, builder rather than just "a worker in wood."

Richard A. Batey, in his *Jesus & the Forgotten City: New Light on Sepphoris and the Urban World of Jesus (Baker 1992)* defines *"tekton"* as "a skilled worker who works on some hard material such as wood or stone or even horn or ivory ... the tasks performed by carpenters and masons could easily overlap".

The Talmud (the 2<sup>nd</sup> century commentary on the first five books of the Old Testament) is often quoted as using the fact that Jesus was a carpenter as an insult, but putting aside attributed references to someone whom the ancient Jews saw simultaneously as an impostor and a threat, the trade of carpenter itself is shown as being deeply respected. According to the scholar Yacob Levy, there is a Talmudic story of a man who arrives in a town looking for someone to help him with a religious problem. He asks for the rabbi, but when he finds that there is no rabbi there, he says, "Is there a carpenter among you, the son of a carpenter, who can offer me a solution?" (cf Yacob Levy, Wörterbuch über Talmudim und Midrachim, Berlin 1924 CE).

This appears to indicate that where there was no rabbi, a carpenter was the person most qualified to interpret law or answer questions.

It is one thing to have a trade and another to have customers. Wood-workers built tools for farmers such as ploughs, yokes, winnowing forks and threshing sledges, and stonemasons built houses, but in a settlement like Nazareth there might not be that much call for such work. However, four miles from Jesus' home town of Nazareth, there was a property boom offering enough employment for a dozen tektons.

The town of Sepphoris was the capital city of Herod the Great's son, Herod Antipas, the client-king of Judea ("client"because he was subject to Rome and ruled under the Emperor). It had been partially destroyed by fire in about 4BCE and during Jesus' youth was being rebuilt into a modern, thriving city. For a carpenter there would be full-time work for years on end. The four-mile walk from Nazareth would be considered a very reasonable commute and the pay more than adequate.

## The Truth about the Nativity

Jesus' birth is also used as evidence of a poverty-stricken start in life.

This story only exists in the Gospel of Luke and it reads (KJV):

"And Joseph also went up from Galilee, out of the city of Nazareth, into Judea, unto the city of David, which is called Bethlehem; (because he was of the house and lineage of David) to be taxed with Mary his espoused wife, being great with child.

"And so it was, that, while they were there, the days were accomplished that she should be delivered. And she brought forth her firstborn son, and wrapped him in swaddling clothes, and laid him in a manger; because there was no room for them in the inn." (Luke 2:4-7).

There is no donkey; no ox; no trailing around Bethlehem, no unkind inn-keepers and not even the slightest hint that Mary was in labor while they searched for somewhere to stay. Even so, the assumption is made that they had to be in a stable because all the rooms in the inns were full.

The word that Luke uses for "inn" is *kataluma* and it is not used in the sense of public accommodations or inn anywhere else in the whole of the New Testament. It means a guest room within someone's personal residence (usually upstairs).

Just before the last supper, in Luke 22:11 Jesus tells the disciples to follow a man into Jerusalem carrying water. He leads them to a house that had a large *kataluma* where they could all gather together for the Passover.

Luke has another story featuring an inn – the story of the Good Samaritan. But there, he doesn't use *kataluma* but *pandocheion*, meaning "a public house for the reception of travellers or strangers." This is an inn, the other refers to staying as guest in a house.

Luke writes that Joseph was of the House of David and had to return to his family's hometown for the census so, given the natural family ties within the Jewish nation, it's more than likely that he had some sort of extended family in the town and common knowledge dictates that no Jewish family would allow even a distant cousin to stay in an inn if he could have stayed in the homes of a relative. Generally the visitors would have been staying upstairs in a guest room but if there was more than one couple staying, there wouldn't have been enough space (the word used in Luke is *topos* – room, space or opportunity) for a woman in labor, so Mary would have been moved out of the guest room and into a place where she could walk, sit, lie down, stretch out and be attended by others while she was giving birth.

This may well have been the room where animals were or had been kept. Animals were frequently kept just the other side of a barrier within the building itself; their body warmth being useful for the family and also to keep them safe from theft. And the stone (not wooden) manger would have made an excellent and secure cradle when the baby was born. I'd say that was evidence of prosperity rather than lack. So, we have to conclude that we cannot possibly know whether or not Jesus was born into poverty. However, the evidence points strongly towards it not being the case at all.

It has often been said that the Church, down the ages, gave the poverty-stricken great hope by saying that there would be a wonderful reward for them in heaven. Equally frequently it has been suggested that the Church wanted all of the money for itself and put out the "jam tomorrow" idea to stop the poor rebelling.

Each is actually a form of resistance. If we truly understand the nature of creative life, we can come to know that we, and only we, decide what is right for us to believe and how prosperous we want to be.

## Chapter Six

# Understanding what you really want

At every workshop I run I ask the participants, "What do you want?" Sometimes people do come up with a definite goal but most often it is a vague non-specific desire.

- To be happier
- To be financially secure
- To be healthier

This is all well and good but these statements are generally followed by a long list of what the participants *don't* want as they tell me their story of why they are not already happier, financially secure and healthier. What they don't realize is that the very telling of their story directly contradicts their desire for healing. They are instructing their Martian to maintain the status quo rather than focussing their energy and intent on what they believe they do want in life.

We all have a story – of loss, lack, pain and grief. But if we repeat it in the now then we simply re-create it in the future. That's the Law of Attraction.

Some people have specific desires – they'd like a home of their own; a decent job; a good relationship/marriage; to be a millionaire; to be famous; to become a powerful teacher or therapist but, again, their follow-on remarks often make it very clear that they are contradicting those desires with their everyday talk of lack in each of these areas.

You simply cannot speak of what you desire and then complain about any aspect of your life and then expect the Law of Attraction to sift out the good from the bad. That is *our* job.

And it takes discipline or at least application to keep our minds on the job of creating what we do want in life instead of bemoaning what we don't want and thus creating it through the repetition of our creative thoughts.

As human beings we were given the unique and amazing gift known as free will so that we and we alone were responsible for the choices we make in our life. Animals don't have free will in the way that humans have. Their choices are dictated by their physical and psychological needs.

No dog is likely to say to itself, "No I won't nag my owner for a walk right now because the weather looks as though it's going to clear up later and we'll both enjoy it more in the sunshine."

No cat is ever going to say to itself, "I realize that other cat is on my territory but I can see that it is old and sick and I can share some of my space as an act of generosity."

Not even one of the higher primates is going to say to itself, "The rest of the tribe is content with the ample food and shelter that we have but I want more. I believe that there is something different to experience; something that will nurture my heart, and I need to go and find it."

Our destiny is to choose. We have the ability, instead of focussing on the story which brought us to where we are now, to decide to set some goals that will take us towards greater happiness.

If you don't have some kind of a plan then you tend to live life by default. And if the world's consciousness is focussed on lack or economic drought then you will be pulled into exactly that reality.

Unless we think consciously from the level of Self, we get what other people are thinking about as presented to us by the news, soap operas, the movies, newspapers and magazines. We all get so tied up in what the world tells us about other people that we start believing it for ourselves.

A belief is simply a thought that has been repeated often

enough by several people. As thoughts become things, the belief then becomes reality. But at any given moment, the thought can be changed.

Fortunately, we are wired to get very clear messages whenever we think something which is not in line with our Soul's purpose. When we are out of line, we feel bad emotionally.

Unfortunately, due to our upbringing, that wiring may have been programmed-over by the desire to please others so that we feel good when we are helping rather than when we are doing something for ourselves.

There's nothing wrong with helping others – this would be a very sad world if there were – but to rely on other people's gratitude rather than our own ability to be in line with our own Soul's purpose is like looking through a mirror at a reflected image instead of experiencing real life.

## Following your bliss

We often find it hard to speak out about our specific desires for fear of the judgment of others and/or our perception of God. This need not be a problem if we follow the simple and glorious suggestion of the American mystic Joseph Campbell who said, "Follow your bliss."

Where it does become a problem is when we haven't a clue what our bliss actually might be!

What is *your* bliss? It has different levels according to our vibrational focus. For the Ego the answer is mostly *security and things*. For the Soul the answer is mostly *freedom and experiences*.

For example, the Ego wants smart, fashionable clothes and a big house and enough money to pay all the bills and buy nice things. When the Ego is infected with the all-too-common childhood programming of "I want doesn't get," it wants a house and money that it can use to help other people. That way it won't be judged as being greedy or grasping.

The Soul wants the feeling of self-appreciation and self-knowledge, the experience of enjoying and sharing the beauty and comfort of a home without any strings attached, it wants new experiences, joyful adventures and the ability to share the knowledge that all is well. There is a subtle but important difference but you can see how easy it is for the Ego to fool us that it is acting at a higher vibrational level than it is.

Here's a quick selection from my friends of what they regard as their bliss:

*Making love, travelling to a new country, having someone to smile at each day, walking a dog, riding a horse, dismantling and re-mantling cars, drinking wine in the bath, prayer, meditation, writing, having a massage, watching a movie with friends, a weekend away on impulse, singing, laughter, eating strawberries or chocolate cake (or both simultaneously), playing with children, gardening, scuba diving, giving and receiving flowers, dressing up to go out, going to weddings and christenings, eating ice-cream, picking blackberries, dancing, kissing in the rain (and the sun and the snow), eating out, drinking champagne...*

Even those who want money (and there is nothing wrong with that) truly want the experiences that they think the money can bring to them.

Step one in attracting what you desire is working out whether you are acting *now* in a way that can bring you your bliss in the future. Most people aren't because they put their pleasures last after the pressures of work, family and other "shoulds."

But remember your Martian who gives you more of the things that you give your attention to: are you giving it a clear message or are you telling it that you are actively seeking stress, obligation and that you and your desires should always come last or not at all?

The Rats in your head will find it very hard to put yourself first.

Start off with doing one action which makes you happy every day and build up from that. It can be as simple as putting jasmine oil in your bath at night. Once the Universe knows that you actually like doing things that are blissful, it will support you in finding out what your ultimate bliss is.

So, as a starting point, make a list of what your bliss may be so that you can start informing your Martian and it can start helping you.

## Long term, medium term and short term goals

Secondly, set yourself some short term, medium term and long term goals. This is important because if you only focus on the long term – happiness, the lovely home and complete security – then it may seem too far vibrationally for you to get to there from here. A good example is the idea of driving from London in England to Rome, in Italy. It's a long way and there will be several days of journeying where you will not be in Italy, let alone in Rome, so it is easy to be discouraged that you are not yet at your destination. So it's a good idea to plan your route and aim for Paris in France, then Geneva in Switzerland along the way.

Suppose that what you really want is a life-long loving partner. You focus on that desire and hold true to it, believing that you are a creator and that if you align vibrationally with the experience of a wonderful relationship. But four weeks later, nothing has happened. It's so easy then to stop believing and drop your vibration with thoughts like, "I asked for my lover but nothing has happened. Where is he? Why isn't it working? I knew it wouldn't work for me..." As soon as you do that, your vibration is lowered and the beloved who is just around the corner recedes.

So it is easier to set short-term and mid-term goals on the way to the life-partner, such as finding some new hobby or social event you attend for its own sake, where you will meet more people. And perhaps joining an on-line dating site or going away on a singles holiday. In the medium term you might think about a home where two people could live comfortably or, if that's not appropriate, make sure that when you buy things or make plans you leave space for the beloved. For example, make sure you have a double bed with pillows on their side; space in your bathroom and wardrobe for their toiletries and clothes, and start expanding your musical, cinematic and other tastes to embrace new experiences. Your future lover may like classical music where you don't now; or they might be a football fanatic where you've never even watched a game; or they might garden while you have never grown a thing. More importantly you need to leave some space and time in your life for someone else. If you don't have something you want, then it's important to embrace the possibility of change in your life to create the opportunity for good to come.

When I was looking for new love, I took up a fencing class which was quite a way from home and not on a public transport route from work. One of my colleagues from work offered to give me a lift there because it was on his way home. It turned out that I loathed fencing and one night when we were driving there, I said would he please drop me off at the bus stop as I'd changed my mind. We got talking about why I didn't like the class and how he had once tried fencing too with the same result.

A few weeks later, it was my birthday. This was the first one since my husband had left me and on the day itself I felt full of grief and anger. The work colleague noticed that I was down and offered to take some work load off my back so I could go out and do some shopping which he thought might cheer me up. While I was out, I saw a poster in a shop window by Jack Vettriano. It was called "Back where you belong" and showed a not-so-young couple embracing passionately at a train station. I went into the shop and bought it and on my return to the office, I showed it to my colleague and told him that I wanted to draw new love into my life. After that, he and I had a drink in the pub a few times. I had the painting on the wall for three weeks before I realized that I had been missing what was right in front of my face – there was a really nice work colleague who was offering me a lot of attention and perhaps this could be what I was seeking. I hadn't noticed before because he wasn't "my type." I plucked up my courage and asked him if he would like to go on a date rather than just a drink and he said yes. He hadn't asked me because he thought I was still in love with my ex, and because he thought he hadn't a chance with me...

He and I have now been happily married for nine years but it's quite likely that we would never even have connected if I hadn't taken that ghastly fencing class!

Discouragement is the very devil of prosperity consciousness. When you set out on your route for Rome there will be unexpected stops and diversions, because you are still working with overcoming the Ego's resistance to your happiness. If you can just overnight in Paris and Geneva and enjoy the experience there without expecting the desired outcome *now* then it will make the route easier.

You cannot get to joy on a road filled with frustration because the whole story is about raising your vibration to the level of how you will feel when you have the required outcome. So making peace with the journey is essential. After all, if you can make the journey a joy then you are already at your ultimate destination – your bliss – even before you achieve your final goal.

Good examples of short term, medium term and long term goals are:

- Finding a night class of something that you could do professionally that you absolutely love.
- Taking the plunge of changing your job.
- Starting your own business.

Or

- Being willing to rent a house somewhere less popular than your desired location so that you have a larger home for a better rent than you would have in a fashionable area.
- Buying a home that has potential for development — still in a less popular area — and working on it yourself.
- Buying your dream home.

In both cases, the business and the dream home may be completely different or located in a new place. You have allowed the process to evolve instead of sticking to the Ego's rules about what, where and when.

Along the way there may be glitches, of course. It may be that the first class doesn't have the perfect teacher so you need to change the class. The job change may be a leap too far for the next step so you have to consolidate. The rented house may challenge your perceptions. But as far as the Martian is concerned, you are firmly en route for Rome. Just don't turn around!

As I was writing this I had a phone call from a friend who is recovering from an operation to remove a cancerous growth. She is frustrated because she is not better yet. This is a woman who had a terminal diagnosis a year ago and who has done wonders in her life to turn it around and dissolve the psychological issues within her that manifested in physical disease.

She is past Geneva now but it has been a long journey and the mountainous route to Rome is getting her down. Even this close she is often tempted to lose hope and turn around. Her inner work on herself has dissolved a whole series of tumours within her whole body so that the cancer receded enough to be operable. But even so, she beat herself up for not managing to dissolve every single tumour.

I'm so glad she did telephone because maybe I could help her to realize how very close to Rome she is and how much fun it can be travelling in the mountains.

## Treasure Maps

These are also called prosperity wheels or dream boards. As it is the nature of the mind to respond to pictures, they are very powerful ways of reprogramming the Ego into accepting new good in your life.

We've already discussed the power of the pictures on your wall so making a prosperity wheel of what you truly want is a very powerful way to bring it to you. The wheel is a visual image of what you want to create which acts as a constant reminder to think about abundance and happiness instead of misery and lack.

Firstly you need to find or buy a large piece of paper or poster board. Strong colors make a stronger impression on the mind. Make the wheel as big and bright and colorful as possible. Drab small images bring drab and small results!

In her book *Open Your Mind to Prosperity* (De Vors) Catherine Ponder suggests the following color schemes:

- Green and gold poster boards for finances, jobs and career success.
- Yellow or white for spiritual understanding and development.
- Blue for education, intellect, writing books or articles or studying for a degree.
- Yellow or orange for health and energy.
- Pink or warm red for love, marriage, happiness in human relationships.

Once you have chosen the color of background which best reflects your goals, find a picture of yourself looking happy and healthy and stick it in the centre of the paper. Some people prefer to put a spiritual symbol there instead of themselves but I find that the prosperity wheel works better with the spiritual symbol placed at the top to help channel spiritual prosperity to you.

Next, work out exactly what you do want in your life, whether it's love, a new home, a car, a job, a holiday, a baby or whatever. This is vital. Prosperity wheels actually work so if you put something on one that you don't really want, you can end up with a problem.

## Words and pictures

Then find color pictures that reflect or represent the things you want in your life and stick them on the paper around your picture. Draw lines from you to the pictures, like the spokes of a wheel, and write on them the embodiment of your dreams, such as "I now have a loving, faithful, kind and honest partner and we love each other." Be sure to write these affirmations in the present tense. Remember how literal the Martian gets – if you want something now, you have to inform the Universe that it is already planning to send it to you.

*Finally, write the all-important Universal Disclaimer on your wheel. This goes as follows: "These things or something better now manifest for me, in easy and pleasant ways, for the highest good of all concerned."*

This is important so that you do not get the cash for that longed-for holiday through a court case or insurance after breaking a leg and you do not get anything which would hurt anyone else. You need to be very clear. Be warned that a prosperity wheel is a very powerful thing and it needs to be made and used with respect. It is vital that you ask for things for the highest good. Otherwise you are practicing magic rather than spirituality and the consequences for you and others could be unpleasant.

## Be careful what you ask for

Be very careful that you only ask for what you truly want! Do not go crazy and put up a picture of Russell Crowe, Jennifer Aniston or any other famous person and ask for them to be the new relationship in your life. It's fine to put their pictures up and to ask for someone *like* them but not for the people themselves. The reason why you shouldn't ask for a specific person, famous or not, is that you have no right to infringe on their free will. It may well be that you might get the person you think you want but miss out on someone much more lovely who looks very like them if you have tunnel vision.

I have drawn amazing things to me through prosperity wheels – and I've made a fair amount of errors when making one. I asked for a sunshine holiday but put up a picture of a woman on her own… I got my holiday – apart from the flights it was even free – but I was rather lonely during it.

Once, when I was wanting to attract love, I put up a picture of a man looking at another woman and omitted to write "single" on the spoke of the wheel leading to it. I attracted a man who was with another woman; who left his partner for me…and consequently left me for another woman.

My ex and I once wanted a larger home in the Midlands of England and we put up a picture of Gleneagles Hotel in Scotland on our dual prosperity wheel because we thought it looked lovely.

Within two weeks we had received an offer from old friends to join them in a venture of buying and restoring an old and very large house in Scotland. Rather swiftly, we took the Scottish picture down and replaced it with one of the kind of house we really wanted! We also added the words "in the Midlands" on the spoke of the prosperity wheel leading to the house – and lo and behold, the perfect home turned up within months.

Another time, I started seeing herons everywhere. It was only when I realized that there was a heron in one of the holiday pictures I had put up that I realized why. The Universe doesn't edit out *anything* on your prosperity wheel and as it was pretty simple for the Martian or the Universe to manifest a heron for me, the birds turned up in droves.

A woman at one of my workshops, said she desperately

wanted a baby and she planned her wheel down to the last detail. But when she came to stick on the picture of the baby itself, she stopped and began to cry. She had suddenly realized she was not ready for a family and that there was work to be done in the relationship with her husband before they went ahead. Without the promise of fulfilment the wheel offered her, she might not have thought the situation through and might have got pregnant too early.

Another participant made herself a "family wheel" to improve relationships with her parents and brother and put a picture of herself holding her baby niece at her christening to indicate family relationships. Five months later she found herself pregnant even though she was using contraception. She had put out a message to the Universe that she wanted to be holding a baby ... so it gave her just what she had asked for. Fortunately she was content with the outcome but it was not what she had expected.

However, the stories I know of successful and happy outcomes of prosperity wheels far outweigh the mistakes. I've seen new jobs, homes and relationships, financial windfalls, new confidence, all of which came for prosperity students who made a wheel.

The most amazing one is the story of a man who was looking for love but didn't have an image of himself for the centre of the wheel. He was a musician and I took a photo of him performing at a New Age fair which he could use. He didn't find love within six months so he threw the wheel in the back of his wardrobe in disgust. Two years later, when he was married with a son, he found the wheel and discovered that there was a poster featuring his future wife on the wall behind him in the picture that I had taken for his wheel!

Another client, who lived in a trailer in an American town, made herself a wheel to find a better home and future for her and her young daughter. She was married to a rich rancher within six months. That marriage did not, ultimately, work out, but the security it gave her enabled her to train for a better job and after she and her husband split up she was able to find work and a lovely home of her own.

Usually a couple of things on your wheel will happen swiftly, as though they were only waiting your permission to manifest. Others take more time – maybe even up to a year. They can only come when your subconscious mind can accept that you deserve them, so there is often more inner work to do.

## Ask only for yourself

Do not ask for things that do not concern you. You may only represent your own desires on a prosperity wheel. It is perfectly fair to put up pictures around you of family loved ones, affirming love and happiness between you, because that is part of your own life. But making a prosperity wheel for someone else without their permission is interference in their life of the highest order.

If a friend or loved one is sick and you want to picture them surrounded by health and love and light, still get their permission first or encourage them to make a wheel for themselves. The only exceptions are if your spouse or your children are too sick to help themselves. Also, do not do a joint wheel for yourself and your partner if they are not 100% committed to the idea with you – and an indication is if they willing to create the wheel with you. Otherwise, their vibration will not be in accord with yours and that will not contribute to a happy outcome.

## Placement

Where you place your wheel is also important. Some spiritual teachers say it should be hidden away so others cannot deride it or interfere with it, and it is certainly true that you should keep it away from anyone who might be rude about it as that criticism will affect how you see it.

However, one woman had one of her dreams come true simply through a friend seeing what she was asking for and revealing that they knew how to achieve her goal. This one is up to you.

However, the Feng Shui of the place in your home, where the wheel is, can be important. There are areas of houses which do not have the correct flow of 'chi' to promote prosperity everywhere. If you do not know the Feng Shui of where you live, your best bet is to put the wheel on the door into a room, or next to the doorway. This is known as "The Gateway of Chi" and is a neutral area which will not interfere with the energies of a wheel.

Finally, look at your prosperity wheel and enjoy the pictures of what you are creating in your life. They will work as long as looking at them makes you feel good.

Change them as they become real or as you realize you no longer need them. When you feel you have had enough of looking at the wheel, take it down and either dismantle it or throw it away and make another one. Don't be surprised if it goes on working long after it has been taken down.

Chapter Seven

# Happiness – at the level of the Soul

*Life, liberty and the pursuit of happiness...* these, according to the American Constitution are our fundamental rights.

But happiness is an odd thing. We may think that we want it but we turn away from it all the time. We think thoughts that make us sad or uncomfortable, we fret about the future and the past and we let those thoughts ruin the present where, really, nothing is wrong.

Sometimes there is a deeply ingrained belief behind such an odd pattern of behavior. It is simply that we believe that happiness is followed by pain and therefore it is easier not to seek joy in the first place but to live in a state of numbness, experiencing life only through the emotions of others on the television, movie screen or through the internet.

This is deeper than the fear that we may love someone and they may walk out on us. It is fundamentally the greatest fear of all – that what we love will die.

And it does. Our beloved pets die; our parents die; our friends die and our partners die. To love means to experience loss. There is no way to escape this fact.

But this is an Ego experience. You see, the Ego is the part of us that truly does die. When we make our transition, the Soul flies home to a dimension to which the Ego has no access. The vibrational level of the Higher Worlds is such that no human Ego can attain it.

No matter what may be right or wrong with religion, it does generally acknowledge that there is a life after death. In an increasingly secular world which is run by Ego, that is simply not true. The Rats in our heads know that when we die, they die.

There will be nothing. No body, no money, no house, no clothes, no drink, no food, no sex, no parties, no cars, no television, nothing physical at all.

With those things we associate laughter, love, relationship, kindness, hope, happiness, but it is not the *things* that bring the experiences that we love or hate; rather the *experiences* that bring the things.

The Soul is the sum total of our experience. And it is our thoughts that bring the experiences. Jack Canfield, the world-famous co-author of the *Chicken Soup for the Soul* series calls it the E+R=O equation. Event + Reaction = Result.

The key is in the reaction. Usually a reaction is just that – a re-action without conscious thought. We react to the news all the time with "Isn't that awful?" and we react to the idea of death with horror. No matter that this strange event will happen to each and every one of us, we nearly always judge it as being wrong.

On 19th June 2006, my husband's and my business partner, Jon Cooper Taylor was going to bed in his London flat when he heard the sound of his 83-year-old neighbour falling over upstairs. He went up to see if she was okay. She was not. A man who had helped her when she fell over in the street the week before had called round; she let him in and he attacked her. Jon told the man to leave but the man then hit the woman in the face again. Jon picked up the telephone and called the police. The man then attacked him with a pair of scissors – and killed him.

How is this a prosperity story? In many ways. But sometimes it takes a gigantic leap of faith to see that. Catherine Ponder, the Unity minister and author of *The Dynamic Laws of Prosperity* (DeVors), had a famous phrase, "I can hardly wait to see the good that comes from this.'"

Firstly, let me say that we grieved deeply along with Jon's family and his other friends. But even though this was a murder – and it made the national news – it wasn't necessarily bad. It's the Ego that wants to make it bad.

Bear with me on this...

Let's look at this as a cautionary tale about the Law of Attraction. Jon was a lovely man; someone who always put other people before himself. He would help anyone at the drop of a hat – and he neglected his own prosperity in order to help others. He told his Martian time, and time again, that other people's lives were more important than his.

He would never take care of himself and he undercharged for everything he did – despite my nagging! Consequently, he was heavily in debt, he rarely got any projects finished and worked all hours of the day and night. He did all the accounts for the elderly people in his flats and he did their shopping for them too. The flats had problems with subsidence, burglaries and several of the people there were sick and needy.

Time and time again he said, "This place will be the death of me." Time and time again we, and other friends, asked him – begged him – to sell up and get out. There was nothing we could do; nothing we could say that would change him. His flat was so filled with clutter that he could barely move. He was very overweight, with thyroid and blood pressure problems, and he told me the week before he died that he had a lump in his back. He had called in a financial expert to look through his finances and work out what he could possibly do. They both laughed when they said that Jon was worth a lot more dead than alive. A few weeks before he died, Lion and I travelled down to London for the surprise 60th birthday party that some mutual friends were holding for him and this big, generous, lovely man wept when he realized how much he was loved.

And so this is his prosperity tale.

He died a hero, saving the life of a neighbour. His estate paid his debts; his son was able to buy himself his first home; his oceans of equipment came to us, to be sifted and passed on to people who needed them ... and we truly believe that Jon is happy at last.

We know he's happy because we can feel him around us – and so can many other people – and because the cyclamen he bought for me when he came to stay one time which had sat neglected and dry in the laundry, bloomed (in June!) with seventeen white flowers.

The man who killed him was jailed for life at the Old Bailey. The police had suspected him of other crimes before but had never managed to catch him; so he's been caught and locked up and that area is a little bit safer.

Jon believed in reincarnation and he used to say that he had been a Viking warrior and also a Crusader. He believed that he had killed many innocent people as a Crusader in Jerusalem and he knew that he had finished his life in those days as a hermit through the guilt. The man who killed him was a Muslim. Jon's astrological chart for the time that he died showed Mars conjunct his natal Pluto (transformation through surgery). It was a red flag moment of choice. Jon chose to engage … to get out of his rut; to live magnificently even if it meant that he lived a very short time. The greatest honour for a Viking warrior was to die in battle.

The last email that Jon sent to me, the day before he died, was a funny one entitled "Funerals are for the Living."

We gave ourselves the most amazing, uplifting, inspiring funeral in Jon's honor and I'm sure he was there appreciating the crowds and the love we extended towards him.

The only thing that has been hard to bear (the grief is not hard) was the attitudes of those who think that the world is an evil place because of what happened to Jon.

Jon chose.

Jon saved his neighbour's life.

Jon protected his neighbourhood from a man already thought to be dangerous.

Jon decided to go home.

Way-to-go Jon!

It makes me cry to write this because I loved Jon and I still miss him very much, but it's a clean kind of grief as it doesn't have anger, resentment or fear within it. And I would rather that this dear man went out swiftly rather than dying slowly (from the health problems he knew about), hopelessly in debt, and overwhelmed by the burden of his duty to others.

Sometimes people ask me how you can have prosperity consciousness in the midst of bereavement. You can. You can see the person's choice to go – to prepare a way – at a time when they have had enough of this world's weight. And you can cry and grieve and let them go, and know that, one day, they'll prepare a table before you where your cup runs over with joy.

Other deaths may be more difficult to deal with than this one. When my first husband died, I had no spiritual or holistic knowledge and that was unbelievably tough.

I'm not trying to say that bereavement is easy ... but the choice we have to make from the Soul is to allow death. To forgive death if you like. Only when we understand that death exists every moment, can we be at peace with the world. We honor the dead by living our life the way we truly want it to be. Even a life ended early can bless us if we allow the grief to lead us to a new perception of love. Even more so if we can forgive.

## Forgiveness

The connection between forgiveness and prosperity makes intuitive sense. At the heart of the prosperous thinking lies the understanding that we live in a "holographic" universe where everything that shows up in our external world is, in some way, a reflection of our own internal states.

The word "forgive" does *not* mean condone. It does not excuse anyone for any wrong they may have done to you; it just releases *you* from the pain. If you break the word down to the old English "fore" as in "before" and give; it translates to "give up that which went before."

I remember seeing the mother of Lesley Ann Downey, one of the children killed by Moors Murderers Ian Brady and Myra Hindley, talking 25 years after the event about how she couldn't forgive them. Of course, what happened to her family was horrific, but you could see in her face and body and the stress that she lived under that she was re-living the pain every day and actually *refusing* to let go of it.

Lesley Ann herself had suffered terribly – and then she had moved on into death and peace. She may even be incarnate again. But her mother's anger was turning in on herself and damaging her even more. She died soon afterwards – a blighted life which could have been transformed by forgiveness. Not by condoning what happened, but by being able to move on and find pleasure in life. She let Brady and Hindley end her life too and that is what we all do when we cannot forgive. The person who hurt us has moved on and probably never gives us a second thought, but we think of them all the time and re-create their cruelty again and again so that we suffer more and more.

Nothing is happening to us *now*. All that is happening is our reaction to the past – and that is the Ego. And it is especially powerful when there is death or a fear of death.

The great spiritual teacher Byron Katie, co-author of *Loving What Is*, (Rider) tells of how she would sit waiting for her daughter to come home, imagining all sorts of horrors happening and fretting until she felt sick. But all that was actually true if she focussed on the present moment was a woman sitting in a chair, worrying…

Forgiveness isn't easy … and it takes time. And God protect us from having to go through anything like what Lesley Ann and her mother suffered. But old hurts *can* be released because very often they are just habits rather than genuine causes of pain. It is *us* not *them* who are hurting ourselves now. The Ego goes over and over old hurts and brings them into the present moment where their constant nagging drowns out the call of our Soul to love and joy.

But how to do it? There are several forgiveness techniques which will work and I'm going to bring in the work of several other teachers here because they all have wonderful techniques. We are all individuals and we hold on to different issues. Not all the following techniques will appeal to you. But please do attempt at least one of them. Old resentments destroy the Soul's calling, and waste lives that could be lived in peace and clarity.

**The Forgiveness List and Affirmations** (Elyse Hope Killoran, Louise Hay and Catherine Ponder)

On a sheet of paper – or more likely, several sheets of paper – begin listing the names (or a general description) of every being (living or dead) and every event and organization with whom you feel any discomfort or irritation.

Scan your life across the decades and remember: the bullies on the school bus, the teacher who gave you a hard time in High School, the friend who betrayed you, the loss of your first love. Don't be surprised if names and events that you have not recalled in years pop up into your consciousness. It is not unusual to experience an emotional response over people and events that you only slightly remember on a conscious level.

It may be easier to write this list in stages, adding names here and there over the course of a few days, until you reach a point where you feel that the list is complete. Remember to include yourself in on the list, and God – because there's a lot of stuff that you're beating yourself up for unnecessarily and even more that originates with religion.

The first time I did this, I was amazed to find more than 130 people and events I needed to forgive. Some of my friends were a bit shocked when I told them that – after all, I've been studying and teaching prosperity for more than 20 years – but it wasn't actually the major needs for forgiveness (parents, lovers etc) who came up as I've done most of the work with them, I was now looking at all sorts of minor issues. But every single one of them was taking up some small amount of space and energy in my Soul. They included a girl who sneaked on me at school for doing something forbidden when I was five; the family doctor who always demanded a kiss when I didn't want to give one when I was six; the mother of a friend who said I had "mousy" hair when I was seven; the maths teacher who shouted at me, also at seven; the girls who laughed when I fell off a pogo stick and broke my arm when I was eight; the cat that slashed and scarred my face when I was nine; the pony who gave me three refusals at the first jump in my first gymkhana at thirteen...

All tiny slights, but worth identifying and forgiving just to free myself from any remaining negativity, and to prevent me from repeating any of the old, forgotten patterns.

Elyse recommends that you take your list out once a day and affirm that you forgive each and every one of the people and events on the list. That's all; you don't have to read it again, just repeat that it is over and the issues forgiven.

Affirmation is a form of repetition of positive statements in the present tense which slowly but surely reprogrammes the reticular activating system. As it learns by repetition, saying good things over and over again will become relevant to the Ego and it will start looking for evidence to prove that they are true.

However, an affirmation will generally only work if you feel good about it. If you don't, the Ego will fight it and maybe even ensure that you forget to do it. There are some beliefs which are too deeply ingrained for a simple "I forgive you" to work when you have invested a great deal of time and emotion into hatred.

Louise L. Hay (*You Can Heal Your Life*, Hay House) recommends "I am willing to forgive" as an easier stage. You can also affirm "I am willing to be free of the past and everything in it."

Or you can just affirm over the paper every day all month that you forgive and bless all those people. It's really worth doing ... and you'll be amazed at how much forgiveness comes your way as a result.

Catherine Ponder's Forgiveness Affirmation is a very long one but it does cover all the bases!

"All that has offended me, I forgive. Within and without, I forgive. Things past, things present, things future, I forgive. I forgive everything and everybody who can possibly need forgiveness of the past or present. I forgive positively everyone. They are free and I am free too. All things are cleared up between us now, and forever. Amen."

**The Pivoting Process** (Teachings of Abraham)

It may be that even the thought of clearing past pain is too much, because you are feeling depression, fear or despair. All of these emotions are paralyzing and all of them stem from a lack of forgiveness for something – probably many things.

Esther Hicks, channelling Abraham, teaches that we have to take baby steps to get out of such debilitating emotions and that it's important to understand the exact steps.

From depression and despair, the next vibrational level is revenge.

From revenge, it's rage.

From rage, it's anger,

From anger, it's frustration.

From frustration, it's hope.

From hope it's much easier...and positivity and forgiveness are possible.

Of course the normal reaction is "I'm not going to allow myself to think about revenge. Revenge is wrong."

And it's also true that moving towards revenge would be inappropriate if you weren't in despair or total depression. And neither Abraham-Hicks nor I am suggesting for one minute that you should act on the feelings of revenge. It's just about a slight vibrational lift out of paralysis for as little as 30 seconds. Because by the Law of Attraction, if you move from one emotion to the next one on the list it will be easier to move on. But if you miss one of the steps out then the jump to the next one can be vibrationally too big to achieve and you sink back into the hopelessness.

However, our friends and families often scupper us as we try to move up the vibrational scale by reacting strongly to any emotion we might feel of revenge or rage. It's not pleasant for them at all to have us ranting in fury. So it's not surprising that people find it hard to lift out of depression. Their own Egos tell them that it's wrong even if someone else doesn't.

When my ex and I split up, I sank into depression and despair. He left at exactly the same time as the dot-com crash which meant that my new business funding had vanished overnight too and I didn't know what to do with any aspect of my life. (you'll see a pattern here very similar to the end of my first marriage). I was also "too holistic" to hand out blame right left and centre because I knew that I must have created this myself and I also didn't want people I knew to judge me as being nasty. So I was trying very hard to be good.

One night, before I'd heard of the Abraham-Hicks teachings, I couldn't sleep and I couldn't cry; I felt totally paralyzed. Something made me decide to go on the internet so that I could see if there was an image on it of the actress my husband had left me for (I was really in a beat-yourself-up phase!). I got out my laptop and began to surf the web. I found a picture of her, which depressed me even more. I noticed that she was playing in a play which was referred to as "a revenge tragedy." Something in my brain sparked and I thought about the idea of revenge. So I put the word into Google and started looking at what other women had done to have revenge on husbands who left them. What I saw shocked me quite a bit but it took me quite neatly through the vibrational stages needed to hope and then to laughter. I found a wonderful site that promised to send a "Toscar" – a golden-colored statue of an Oscar playing with himself – anonymously to anyone you wanted. It seemed so appropriate that I made plans to do it in the morning and went really quite peacefully to sleep. In the morning, of course, it seemed ridiculous but I did feel better. And that was certainly the turning point in my recovery.

**Ho'oponopono** (Morrnah Nalamaku Simeona and Dr Ihaleakala Hew Len)

This is a Hawaiian technique which is only fully taught in workshops but there is a truncated form, as taught in Joe Vitale's book *Zero Limits* which is incredibly effective in helping with forgiveness processes and which I wholeheartedly recommend. It works very simply, by understanding that all our problems are caused by the data in our Egos. That data is the source of all unhappiness and pain. Just like a computer, you can reprogram that data and the Ho'oponopono way is to repeat the phrase "I love you, I'm sorry, please forgive me, thank you," to yourself over and over again until you are virtually saying it in your sleep. This simply dissolves hurtful data and allows good to flow to you. It will help you forgive without even thinking about what you need to forgive. You will find in times to come that you remember something that used to cause great emotion with none at all.

Finally on forgiveness, a quotation from psychologist and angel expert Doreen Virtue: "Forgiveness is different from saying 'I lose,' or 'I was wrong and you are right.' It is different from letting someone off the hook for a perceived wrong. Forgiveness is simply a way of freeing your spirit and becoming an unlimited being. Peacefulness and increased energy are the prizes, and forgiveness is the price. To me, it's a bargain."

# Chapter Eight

# Debt and the Pay-Off

What is debt? What really counts as debt? What is good debt and bad debt?

A mortgage is a debt ... but nobody feels inferior or guilty about having a mortgage ... and others aren't judgmental about those who do have them even though the word means "hold until death" in French. In fact, to fit in with the Social Ego you need to own a house which means that you will most likely have a mortgage. So a mortgage is seen as a "good debt." It confers status.

In the UK owning a house only became such a social requirement in 1980s when the then Prime Minister Margaret Thatcher encouraged people to buy their council houses. In many parts of Europe, renting is considered just as valid an option. In fact, to rent a house means that you are taken care of by the agent or landlord if something goes wrong and that can be seen as great prosperity.

The idea that renting is "throwing money away" assumes that money is a finite thing. By the Law of Attraction, it will only be finite if you think it is. As a Universal energy resource, it is endless.

A car loan or hire purchase is also a debt. Not a lot of people worry about those. The product bought with the loan will probably confer status on the owner but it's not considered as "good" a debt as a mortgage.

Countries have debt. We don't sit up and worry about the national debt (although the news does tend to point out what a very bad thing it is). We fuss a bit about Third World Debt and we want governments to forgive them.

But credit card debt and loans to cover credit card debts are considered *bad debt*!

Why? Because we are told they are bad, and consequently believe they are bad, and that belief makes us feel uncomfortable because we feel that we are somehow bad people for not being able to handle our money properly. But if you think about it, the vast majority of debt is greatly to the advantage of the lender. They are making more money from you than you actually owe. So lenders at least think that your debt is a good thing.

It probably doesn't help here if you dislike the people who lent you the money because they make a profit on it!

In Islam, any transaction or loan where the payment of an additional amount on the principal amount is made conditional to the advance of such a loan is called *riba* and is forbidden. Islam considers interest to be a socially unjust mechanism for lending money that benefits the rich to the detriment of the poor, as it does not involve any investment risk for the lending party. If Muslims receive interest money from a bank account it is generally recommended that this money is given to a charitable cause with the understanding that there is no return on the donation. The money should be used by the charitable organisation to help the poor and needy, but is not to be used for specific projects including the construction of mosques.

There's no doubt that being in debt carries with it a definite feeling of weight and I know that in the days when I was heavily in debt and I didn't understand the Law of Attraction, life felt very hard and unfair. There seemed to be no way out either.

So, given that we create our thoughts, emotions and beliefs, why would we create debt? Could it be that there is a pay-off? Everything we create has a pay-off – every relationship issue; every disease; every money problem.

Have a think about it ... what can you do better while being in debt? Or perhaps, more accurately, what can you avoid doing by being in debt?

There must be something. If your Ego is quite creative enough to make a problem of the fact that you *are* in debt; it's quite capable of finding some good in there too. However, it might not tell your consciousness about this particular hidden benefit.

Could it be that while you're in debt you can't afford the clothes that would make you look good? You can't have the car that would make you feel good? Could it be that while you're in debt you can't fulfil your life's path? Could it be that you don't have to stick your head above the parapet? That no one has to envy you while you are in debt? That you have every excuse for *not* doing things that would enhance your life?

So in prosperity terms, what is debt? It looks as if it's about getting more than you can afford right now. But sometimes we get into debt just to eat and pay the rent, so that can't be all there is to it.

Let's play with that a bit – perhaps debt is saying something about giving out more than you are capable of doing; of making commitments and promises to others that are, ultimately, going to drain you and even make you ill.

Do you do that elsewhere in your life too? Do you put others first to your own detriment? If so, then the practice of tithing (see earlier) will be a great help as long as you remember to put your tithes into your inspiration and celebration boxes first.

Debt has many levels; the first and most basic level is self-punishment.

Secondly, there is punishing others. Your parents? Your partner? Proving to them that you can't or won't be free of something; that you aren't willing to make them proud by succeeding? And is there anyone who you feel would be a drain on you if you were financially secure? Be honest.

Thirdly there is fear of freedom. Every minute that you worry about debt, you are creating the future in the light of what you can't do because of lack of money. Why would you want to do that?

To get out of debt would leave you free to do what you want with your money. Some part of you doesn't want the responsibility of that; it seems safer to be in slavery. Why is it easier to be beholden to others than to be in full charge of your life? Why do you not want to be free? Why is freedom so frightening? Is it the amount of choices you have to make? Is it a fear that you would mishandle your freedom? Is it just safer not to try?

Who would you be without that limitation? Who would you be if you genuinely believed that you were wealthy and in credit?

The only place that debt can be resolved is in your mind. You started the debt; you can end the debt. Are you brave enough to face a future without debt? Are you prosperous enough to release the fear around debt; to let debt go?

Debt is also about not being able to fulfil the demands of others and feeling guilty about it. This means that we have signalled to the Universe that we are not taking enough time for ourselves; by over-working; or it may signal a general lack of self-esteem about how much you give out, how much you expect in return.

When I was in my twenties I always used to be £4,000 in debt with bank loans and credit cards (that's probably equivalent to about £15,000 in debt now). It felt totally normal to me and I didn't worry about it because I had a salaried job and I made the minimum monthly payments.

When I married Henry, he paid the debts off for me, saying it was silly to be paying interest – that was in the days before credit cards offered 0% interest.

When Henry died and I began to do more than just survive again I became a freelance magazine writer and earned quite well – but guess what, the debt came back; it just crept up on me. The real reason for it was that my Ego was used to my being in debt; it felt "right" to me.

And guess how much debt it was? Yep, £4,000.

Then my Dad died and left me his car – which was worth how

much? Yes, £4,000. So I cleared the debt. And somehow it crept back up on me again.

When I married for a second time it was to a man who had very similar financial issues to mine and our joint debt rose considerably.

When we broke up I ended up £12,000 in debt (the equivalent of that old £4,000) and as I allowed my professional world to fall apart simultaneously (do you notice a pattern here?) the debt just grew and grew.

The point of this is that debt is a habit; it becomes engrained in a way if you've had it for a while. It's engrained in the national psyche too – your country is in debt. Every time the news points out that the average debt in the UK is £15,000 per capita it encourages the collective unconscious to believe that this is a good idea. And of course, for the Economy, it is a VERY good idea. Anything that gets us spending creates economic growth.

One thing I do suspect is that your unhappiness increases in line with your debt – or your level of debt increases in direct line with your unhappiness.

## The secret of dissolving debt

The great secret of getting out of debt is to treat the existing supply as the desired supply. Instead of griping about what we don't have, we need to start some consistent appreciation of what we do have even if it seems to have nothing whatsoever with money.

The money just represents our level of vibration and energy. Bad debt means bad-feeling energy. Turn the energy around and debt begins to dissolve.

People at workshops often look at me blankly when I talk about being grateful for what they have. I ask them to come up with 50 things in their life that they truly appreciate and they can just about manage a dozen. They are showing quite clearly why they are in financial or emotional difficulties. If they are informing their Martian that they have nothing to be grateful for, It *can't* give them anything that they could appreciate.

If you have sight, hearing, a sense of smell, a sense of taste and a sense of touch, you have a thousand things to be grateful for. Maybe the issue here is the word "gratitude" which may bring in childhood resentment at being told to be grateful for things you didn't want! The word "appreciation" is easier. It also helps to try and move as much as you can out of the Ego consciousness of *things* into the Soul consciousness of *experiences*.

So think about ten things you love to see; ten favourite songs or pieces of music; ten wonderful scents; ten things you love to eat; ten things you love to touch and you've got 50 appreciations before you even start. Here are a few suggestions:

**Sight:**
Sunrise or sunset
Stars
The first snowdrops
Ice on a cobweb
Wind rippling golden corn

**Sound**
Your favourite piece of music
The dawn chorus
The sound of ice clinking in a drink on a hot day
Someone you love saying your name
The sound of a waterfall

**Smell**
The scent of a fragrant rose
The scent of fresh laundry
The scent of freshly-mown grass
The scent of coffee
The scent of the sea

**Taste**
Chocolate
Your favourite meal
A sun-kissed peach
Chips
Cool, fresh water

**Touch**
The feel of a beloved animal's fur
The feel of velvet
Crisp fresh sheets on your bed
Warmth on your skin
The feel of a hug/kiss

If you can feel the experience as you think of the things you appreciate, you add energy to the good vibration. It's not a cop-out or a denial of whatever else is going on in your life to think of things you love and that make you feel good. Rather, it's a way of ensuring that the future is a better one.

When my beagle Didcot died, I missed her very much and grieved as only a dog-loving softie can. She had been with me through some pretty testing times and bringing her back from the USA as the first dog in on the Passports for Pets scheme had been an incredibly powerful experience.

I needed to grieve before considering getting another dog; and (money again) I thought that I couldn't get another beagle at the time as they cost £800 and I wasn't rich enough at the time. I'm a beagle fanatic so any other kind of dog was not appealing. And anyway I was working three days a week at the BBC so it wouldn't be fair on a puppy.

I did register on a beagle breeder's site saying that I'd be interested in a puppy in about a year's time as a kind of affirmation that I would be able to afford one then.

In the meantime, as a part of my morning meditation I would

imagine myself holding Didcot on my lap, stroking her and remembering just how her fur felt and how it lay on her body, inhaling her scent, seeing how lovely she was in her prime at about seven, and feeling the weight of her, the way she would lean on me for a cuddle and enjoying a whole doggy fantasy experience.

I did this for about two weeks and found great comfort in it. Yes, sometimes I would cry too, but it was better to get that bit of emotion out rather than suppressing it. Then one morning as I was actually doing my beagle meditation the telephone rang. I let it ring but the lady calling started leaving a message on the answer phone about beagles so I picked up and it was the breeder I had registered with. She said she had had a prospective owner for one of her puppies drop out at the last minute and although I'd said I didn't want a beagle right now, she'd wondered if I would change my mind.

It was tempting but unrealistic so I told her so. Then she said, "Would you consider an older dog?"

When I asked her what she meant she said that she had a seven year old bitch who had been a show dog and then a breeding bitch.

"I always try to retire them to loving homes so that they can be cosseted and have a wonderful old age," she said. "Would you be interested?"

"How much is she?" I asked cautiously.

"Oh, free of course!" said the lady. "I'd never charge to get one of my girls a good home."

So, our lovely dog Puzzle came to us two weeks later, a dear, sweet, loving girl in her prime. She came because my Martian knew that I was focussing on loving a beagle of that age, seven years old … so it had to give me one.

## Become a millionaire in your mind

Debt and poverty consciousness form a vicious circle. So act as if you were a happy millionaire each and every day. I don't mean buy a dozen cars or jet off to the South of France; I mean walk like a millionaire; dress like a millionaire (maybe one who's having a casual day); smile like a millionaire; enjoy life like a happy millionaire. Make a feast out of every meal, even if it's beans on toast. Clear and lay the table properly; sit down and appreciate each mouthful. Have a beautiful home; fill a vase or a carton with flowers or foliage if you have a garden. Pretend. Pretend. Pretend. That's all your mind does anyway – it makes pictures of the horrible things that could happen. Why not make pictures of the lovely things that could happen instead?

How would you act if you *were* a millionaire? People say airily "oh, money wouldn't change me," but it would. It would mean that you weren't afraid to go into expensive shops and browse; you'd look at the most expensive holidays in the travel agent and you'd ask estate agents for brochures for lovely houses. So do those things. Looking is free but it tells the Martian that you are looking up instead of down. For years before we were able to buy our lovely home, I regularly got brochures of houses that we would like but did not have the financial energy to purchase (at that time). It raised the game and so the Martian raised it too.

Make a millionaire prosperity wheel of all the things you would do if you were a millionaire; fantasise about hiring a Caribbean island for a month and flying everyone you love out there first class for a holiday. You could test drive an expensive car or have a personal shopping session at an expensive department store. Those sessions are free and you don't have to buy anything. If you feel uncomfortable or a fraud doing that, then it's telling you clearly that your energy level is too low for prosperity and that's why you're broke. Genuinely wealthy people wouldn't have a problem trying but not buying.

An easier step is to dress up. I'm a natural-born scruff and I work from home but every working day I put on make-up, arrange my hair becomingly and don a pair of diamond earrings.

I make sure that I look good enough to answer the door as though I were a millionaire. At the weekend I relapse into scruffiness – as do so many millionaires…

The diamond earrings are a prosperity story too … I had wanted a simple pair of diamond studs for a while but I hadn't made the decision to buy any as it seemed a bit extravagant. Then Lion and I went on holiday to the Dominican Republic and several comments on the website where we booked the holiday said it was a good idea to take unwanted jewellery to the island as the local woman who worked at the hotels loved to receive jewelry instead of tips. I had a lot of old stuff in my jewelry box that I didn't want; some precious jewelry but mostly not and so I took a small bag of jewelry to the Dominican Republic.

As it turned out, the advice appeared to be wrong or there just didn't seem to be much opportunity to give the stuff away. Just before we headed back, the holiday rep gave us some unusual advice: she said we should not carry any jewelry in our carry-on luggage as there were a rash of pick-pockets at the airport. Instead, it should go in the hold.

I obeyed her and when we got home, we discovered that my suitcase had been forced open and the little bag of jewelry had been taken. Nothing else had gone including some things that were of greater value.

The insurance company gave us a new suitcase and, on my descriptions of the pieces of jewelry taken, they gave me credit for £450 at a local jewellers. So I went and bought a pair of diamond ear studs.

This *is* a story of the Law of Attraction because I fully intended my tatty jewellery to go to people in the Dominican Republic so the Universe ensured that it did – and it gave me the opportunity in return to have what I really wanted.

What's more, two months later, a friend gave me a second pair of diamond ear studs. She had just bought a better pair and remembered my saying once that I would like a pair of diamond studs. So then I had two pairs!

I recommend that you read a very old story, *The Little Princess* (Wordsworth) by Frances Hodgson Burnett. It's a children's book about a little girl reduced to abject poverty who pretends that she is a princess, and so she acts with courtesy and dignity towards everyone. She pretends that the attic she lives in is a beautiful, luxurious room fit for a princess, and she pretends that she is loved and appreciated.

And the Universe believes her ... and shows up with the goods. I love children's stories like that; they are so powerful and simple – and they are messages from God to all children, whatever our age.

So pretend that you live a life without debt. That the Law of Attraction has paid it off for you and that there is no need to worry any more. Of course, pay your instalments (with love and gratitude) but act and live as if the Universe has taken it all away.

## Make peace with the debt

By making debt wrong we are at war with it and you cannot solve anything through war. As the Abraham-Hicks teachings point out, we have a war on terrorism, a war on drugs, a war on cancer, a war on knives, a war on crime. The more we focus on warring against something, the more attention we give to it and the larger we make it.

Making peace with debt is quite simple; you bless it. Every time you receive a credit card statement, write "I bless you and release you and move forward into prosperity" on the statement. Do the same with your bank statement if it's in overdraft.

Make peace with the utility companies. Make peace with the mortgage lender and the landlord; make peace with the council, and make peace with yourself.

As long as you hate something, it will grow. If you bless it and release it, then it can dissolve. Write "with love and thanks" after you write out the amount whenever you write out a cheque instead of "only." Draw hearts and flowers on the cheque too ... it changes the energy around your payment.

I once got a parking fine when I was doing something I didn't want to do at Christmas time. Of course, in line with how negatively I felt, I had parked illegally. It was really hard to write that cheque with "with love and thanks" on it when I was so cross about it. In the end I decided to be silly and covered the cheque with glitter, angels, snowmen and pictures of presents and stars. That made me feel much better. The fines department didn't cash it for more than a month – by which time the Universe had covered the debt for me! Perhaps it cheered them up receiving a cheque like that.

### Show up for the Muse

Showing up for the Muse is a concept from Steven Pressfield's excellent book *The War of Art* (Orion). If you are creative (and all human beings are creative in some way) then your purpose in life is to follow your bliss as a creator.

Being in debt often stops this: it's so tempting to believe that you can't be creative because you are in debt (and that's a nice trap by the Ego to prevent your trying).

But if you ensure that just for five minutes a day you do what you were born to do, whether it's sing, write, bake cakes, walk, draw, whatever, then you are on the road to beating debt.

Here's a clue: Your life's purpose is NEVER about taking care of another person. Even if you are a natural carer or parent, the joy is about creating something that YOU can do with that person; not about caring for the other in itself. If you do what makes you shine, you become an inspiration rather than a prop.

The passion for caring for others can also an Ego trick. Yes, of course we must look after each other, but we must look after ourselves *first*. Otherwise we have no good energy for the others and everyone ends up dragged down.

Visualize yourself in the Maldives; create your own recipe

book; start writing that novel; enter a karaoke competition (or a TV talent show); do whatever you can to move towards your life's goal. The task is not to wait until everything is perfect before you start living – but to live so that everything can become perfect.

If you don't know your life's goal, that's part of the problem. At workshops I often ask people to write a couple of paragraphs of their own obituary if they had died today. Then I ask them to write the perfect obituary should they drop dead from perfect health at 108 having lived the life of their dreams. That helps them focus on what they would truly like to have been and done.

It's very good to tell your Martian that at the end of your lifetime, you will have had years of being happy and lucky in love; you will have taught your children wonderful prosperity principles so that they are thriving too; you will have lived a life of abundance; you will have been of service to humanity and nudged the world an inch or two into becoming an even better place.

### Get a plan.

Affirmation is different from denial. Denial is when you ignore what is happening. Affirmation is observing what you have already created and starting to create something you prefer.

Denial never helps. Getting a financial strategy for paying off debt instead of wallowing in it or ignoring it, does help. If you bank on the internet, send the odd £5 off to the debt every time you have it spare. Even £1 makes a commitment to being back in credit.

Fill in a pay-in form for your bank account with £1,000,000 or whatever amount you like. For the signatory, write "The Universe" and place the form in your wallet.

Make up five affirmations of how you want to live and then write down the list, as if it already is, on a series of cards, and read it out loud to yourself every night and every morning. Put emotions in the list too, such as the fact that you are loving being happy and prosperous and enjoying your work. That will help to create the focus you need to start the journey.

Don't worry if your desires change each day to start with, that's your mind sifting and sorting what you really want from what you may think you want. If you persevere, you'll get a core list for your planning session and within a month, you will have some strong, focussed goals, and some signs that what you truly want is on its way to you.

An example of your list might be:

- I am loving earning £500 a day at work I adore doing.
- I'm so enjoying my wonderful Five Star holiday in Antigua.
- I'm so happy feeling prosperous in every moment.
- I'm loving being in love with my perfect partner – and being loved just as much in return.
- I'm truly enjoying my wonderful, comfortable life in my perfect home.

When you've read all five, say something at the end along the lines of:

"In return for these blessings I am happy to give the best possible service I can as (your chosen work) demonstrating joy and prosperity in the world.

"I know that these things, or better, are mine and that they are now manifesting for my highest good. I can see them with my eyes, I can touch them with my hands; I can feel them in my bones.

"Everyday I am being given the ideas to manifest all this joyfully and efficiently.

And so it is."

So put your everything into enjoying the moment – feeling good in the now – and watch how the experiences mount up and make you feel richer at all levels. And while you're becoming rich, your bank account will start to reflect that for you too.

## Conflict and Contrast

There are basically two ways of waking up in the morning: the first way is when you say, "Good Morning God!" and the second is when you say "Good God, it's morning..."

The second is, generally, the more common of the two. The Ego runs mostly on fear and guilt (there's anger too but that's usually based on one of the other two emotions) and it sees another possible day of conflict ahead.

So often, we fear that the day will be ghastly; that we won't be able to do what we have to do; that we'll do it wrong and that others will judge us. We are afraid that we won't have enough money, time, love, talent or luck.

Guilt cracks in second and hits on the stuff that we haven't done already that we think we ought to have done – and that just adds to the fear.

The conflict is in us – we are het up even before we see or speak to another person and we fuel our discomfort by checking emails, opening mail, or dealing with telephone calls before we have taken time to focus ourselves and tell the Martian what kind of a day we would like to have.

Wouldn't it be lovely to wake up on a day when there was no conflict whatsoever? Impossible, I'm afraid.

The day that we are completely without conflict we will ascend from the Earth. Life is a continual state of growth and that cannot be done without some form of conflict. But conflict doesn't have to be bad.

It's conflict to open your eyes in the morning – your eyelids have to work against air pressure and there's pressure between the lids and your eyes, eased by fluid. Those conflicts are tiny but anything that rubs together causes conflict. It's conflict for a new seed to open and push its way through the earth to grow into the light. It's conflict when you bite into an apple or tread on grass.

Conflict is a fact of life on this planet. That does not mean life needs to be painful, depressing, angry or competitive; it means that there is always conflict around us which will touch us. Whether it is conflict in the Middle East, a feeling of discomfort over our relationship with your mother-in-law, or an irritation with your partner over the washing up, it is how you react to that conflict which is important.

You can choose to ignore it, be angry with it or to deal with it and pass on. The Source invented conflict. It's part of the deal. Without it we wouldn't have fire, cars, gardens, houses, sex. Even a kiss is friction as two mouths need to put pressure on each other. It's just the degree of conflict and the perception of it that is the issue.

But perception is all. And for most of us the word "conflict" refers to angry exchanges or irritation. It can help to refer to it as "contrast" rather than conflict.

### Giving attention to harmony

We certainly get less painful conflict in your life if we choose to give our attention to harmony within and around us rather than focussing on the reported conflict in the external world. The Law of Attraction *has to* draw conflict to you if you give a great deal of attention to it on the news and if you are emotionally affected by them, even if you watch fictional conflict in soap operas and dramas.

You can only be drawn to the idea of viewing the external conflict if there is already conflict in your own heart and mind. If we were not at war within ourselves there could be no war outside us and we would not be interested in seeing it expressed externally. It follows that as we all, as individuals, clean up our prosperity consciousness, we actually do help world peace. Sometimes people say that prosperity work is selfish; for this reason alone, it is the most unselfish thing that you can do.

Each of is affected differently by external images of pain, war or discord, according to our personal psychological make-up. Fiction affects everyone to varied degrees. Someone who has a great deal of water in their astrological chart is always swayed more than someone with a great deal of fire, air or earth. I know one man with a totally dry chart who finds soap operas amusing and who can watch any amount of violent movies without taking any of it in or projecting it out. But another (Cancerian) man is totally drawn into the plot developments of his favourite soap. He is always attracting emotional scenes in his life whether it's with family or just someone in the queue at the bank. Only you know what affects you according to your emotions when you view it. If you find yourself pulled in and experiencing emotion, then you are engaging in conflict and the chances are you will create it in your own life.

Most, if not all, personal conflict is simply Ego disagreement. That doesn't mean that it's not profound nor serious. The Ego constantly seeks to find evidence that it is right so someone coming along with a different point of view can be very scary. When that point of view claims to have a different or better God or if it wants to take some of your land, then we have the basis of war.

The Soul has a different view; it can accept other people's contrasting and conflicting views as equally valid and it doesn't see the need to react to them or change them.

Jewish mysticism taught me that the Soul knows that there is enough for all and that nothing can truly threaten it unless it sinks to the level of Ego and defends itself. Of course living that life to the full would make someone a modern-day saint.

## Thoughts of conflict

The author and teacher Byron Katie teaches that it is only our thoughts that hurt us and that defensiveness is the first act of war. That's a hard one to embrace but it's worth considering. No matter what the other person does, it is your reaction that escalates conflict. Of course it's virtually impossible to see how one could not resist or defend when there has been a real attack but we need to pull back on that one and consider why the attack has been made on us. How did we attract it? If the outside world is a reflection of the world within, the best we can do for the world at large is clean up our own act and that means looking at our own conflict.

There is a valid spiritual view that even natural disasters are tied up with humanity's thought forms.

It would make sense that if the Earth is a cosmic angelic being as taught by many modern interpretations of ancient traditions, then it will respond to our thoughts and feelings. So global warming could be caused just as much by anger as by physical causes, and natural disasters could be the Earth scratching the itch that is humanity's almost constant state of frustration and irritation. So maybe you do more to contribute negatively to pollution and global warming by bitching about the driver of a 4x4 than the driver of that car is doing...

But for the moment we are not concerned with outside situations – the whole idea is to understand that it's all about *us*, not about *them*.

Would it be nice if there were no contrast/conflict? In theory, yes. But life is like a buffet. Without alternatives it would be very boring. We have all the options available and get to choose what we want. Our Ego says that the only choices it wants are things that it already likes, but you know what, not having the opportunity to change our mind, expand and grow would make us very limited. I have a subscription to a digital music station and it often offers me music that I don't like. All I have to do is click "next" – I don't have to get that artist banned from the station or exterminated, which is what we have a tendency to do when we don't like something in life. It's up to us to choose. It is not up to us to try and get the range available at the buffet reduced.

If I refuse to listen to that artist for long enough, the station offers him or her less frequently and all I have to do is click "next". Eventually, it doesn't offer that music at all. I didn't have to fight to get it removed; I just did not listen to it so it stoppped presenting what it noted I didn't like. And if I want to listen to that previously-disliked music at any future time, it can be reinstated into my play list any time I like. And sometimes, if I let the music that I thought I didn't like, play without clicking "next", I find it's not so bad after all. Sometimes I even get to like it.

My father always offered me onions when he was serving up a casserole for lunch. For sixteen years I said, "No, I don't like onions," and got irritated that he never seemed to remember. But then one day I ate onions at a friend's house (to be polite) and discovered that my tastes had changed. So next time my father asked if I wanted onions, I said, "yes please" and he wisely gave me some without any comment.

If the Universe had simply not made onions a possibility for me after sixteen years of refusal, my life would have been much the poorer, not to mention my cooking skills. And imagine if I had had the power to stop onions from appearing in my world at all. That would have meant no onions for anyone who was in contact with me even if they liked onions.

I don't personally watch soap operas – I have to be very careful about what I watch and listen to my astrological chart is very watery. But I wouldn't disallow other people from watching soap operas or say they should be banned. That's none of my business. I can always choose not to watch them and if I think there's nothing else on the TV then I can always read a book or talk to a friend. And it's perfectly possible that someone watching a soap opera would be inspired or helped by something in it even if it's only how *not* to act or behave!

You only get inspired by contrast. Life experience gives you the desire for something more and something different every time you experience conflict. And by focussing on the desire rather than the cause of the conflict, your vibration rises.

As we harness the Law of Attraction, we draw to us more and more of what we want and less and less of what we don't want, but the Universe will always offer us choices in order to develop our choosing skills. When we object to that and focus on the thing that we do not want instead of just saying, "no thanks, not for me," we are heading for the negative side of conflict.

## Conflict and Relationships

I once studied some Essential Peacemaking work between men and women. It was based on the work of Danaan Parry and Jerilyn Brusseau and it taught me that conflict is impossible without a relationship between the opposing parties. It may not be a loving relationship – it may just be a stone and a shoot battling it out for who gets that bit of location – but it is a connection.

In humans, wherever there is disagreement it is because of differing Ego opinions and you are having a relationship with someone with whom you disagree just as you are with someone you like. Energetically you are strongly linked to them, and the more you dislike or hate them, the stronger that link becomes. Resolution of any conflict always deepens the relationship because it has the potential of raising it from the Ego to the level of the Soul.

Virtually every communication between humans is either an offer or a request for love in some form. An angry demand for your attention is an unskilful request for love. An insistence on giving you something you don't want is also a request for love, just one that is disguised as an offering. That's why giving is such a complex subject. So many people who think they are givers are actually demanders. "If I give you this, you will be grateful to me and that will make me feel good about myself."

Conflict resolution is not about problem solving. Once one problem goes another may come. It is about resolving the need between people to create problems.

Byron Katie is one of the best teachers of how to resolve conflict within ourselves and in our relationships with others. Her four questions will work for nearly every single issue in life. You can find Byron Katie on *YouTube* practicing what she calls "The Work". The outcome of her "turnaround" technique is to take consciousness from Ego to Soul to see that the beliefs that hurt us are our own illusions. She also teaches that there are three kinds of business: my business, your business and God's business.

Conflict comes when we interfere in other people's business (and that includes God's). Whenever we think someone should get a job, a life, a new attitude, a new partner, a new coat, that they should take better care of themselves, stop being such a bitch to us, or understand what we want from life, then we are in their business. We can't rule or decide what they think, we can only deal with our own thoughts and, if we believe in ourselves, their attitudes, jobs, clothing or thoughts can't hurt us.

*We* hurt us. Only we hurt us – by reacting through Ego to other people's business.

## Is it any of my business?

When we fret about famine, earthquakes or war, we are in God's business. We don't know what's really going on anywhere else but inside us (and sometimes not even that!) and whenever we get lost in other people's business or God's business we feel disconnected, lonely, frightened and separate. Those feelings, to the Ego, are hell because in the middle of them, its job is still to try and prove that we are right. And if we are right, then everyone else must be made to be wrong. Making people wrong takes a lot of time and energy (although internet forums make it a lot easier nowadays). And if we are spending our time in other people's business, and God's business, who is home taking care of our business? No one.

No wonder our life doesn't work; no wonder our relationships flounder! We're too busy being in our partner's business or our boss's business to be the person they originally fell in love with or hired.

In conflict it is vital to get back into your own business. By defending, you are in *their* business. Okay, it may take a Guru-level of consciousness to respect yourself and do everything you can do to be balanced and comfortable in the face of hostility. But it is the goal of the Soul. That's why the Ho'oponopono technique of reciting "I love you, I'm sorry, please forgive me, thank you," as a mantra is so powerful. It is coming from the level of the Soul and it is pulling you back into your business and encouraging the other person to get into their business instead to trying to push into yours. In a way it is your Soul being the mother who is comforting and loving the Ego so that it doesn't need to be defensive.

Even doing Ho'oponopono non-verbally in a conflict situation will help to resolve any situation. It changes the vibration of your aura or electro-magnetic field and dissolves the cords that are psychically pulling your opponent's hair out. As you change vibrationally they must, by Law of Attraction, also change their vibration or, if they won't, they will feel very uncomfortable in your energy field and will have to move away. Sometimes they move right out of your life and if you hold that higher vibrational energy, they will never be able to offer you disrespect again – because you no longer believe that they can.

Danaan Parry and Jerilyn Brusseau's Essential Peacemaking teaches that everyone needs a comfort zone, a place or a token of safety where their Ego can curl up and recover or rest when conflict gets too much. If we can hold onto something that brings thoughts of love and security, and where no one else can reach us emotionally or physically, then the Ego can feel calmed and appreciated. There's no point in getting angry with ourselves – we couldn't even walk without the Ego-consciousness within us, let alone get dressed or feed ourselves. It's only doing what we, and others, trained it to do.

Spiritual growth can be a tiring business and we all need our comfort zone.

It can be a place, a crystal, a picture, a colour, a piece of music or even a bar of chocolate, or all of them together. It is something or somewhere that you love and feel confident about and where conflict does not intrude. You can hold it in memory or have a token of it to hand; it's not always possible to go to an actual place.

I have two very important comfort zones. One is a picture of an 8-ft barracuda which I can click on by going to the desktop on my computer. That works because I was once in a rather worrying situation with an 8-ft barracuda off the Great Barrier reef in Australia. Not only did I survive the encounter but I got very definite guidance from above as to how to survive it. So the picture reminds me that God/Spirit has got me out of worse situations than any I may find myself in now.

The other is my wedding ring. It's made of beaten gold and I love it. Again, it reminds me that I've overcome some awful and frightening things and that I am loved, and that this ring is linked to the identical ring on the finger of the man I love most in the world, and that whatever I do, he loves me and will hold me close.

You need to be within reach of whatever your place of security is, through a token or a picture or a memory, to feel strong enough not to engage when someone near you is conflicted and projecting their feelings of conflict onto you. If you are miles away from that safety zone either physically or emotionally, there may be too much fear for you to react clearly to conflict. Always make sure you have access to whatever represents your safe haven when you know there is recognizable conflict ahead. And if you're caught on the hop, then retreat until you can access a clear memory of the safety zone or until you feel more comfortable. Going into a difficult business situation, have something representing the comfort zone in your bag or pocket so that you can touch it. If you can remember to find that safety zone/ crystal/ tune/ ring/ memory in the midst of conflict, then you can respond from a conscious (Soul) place, instead of simply being reactive (Ego).

Even more, you become conscious that love/hope/resolution exists. It is easy to run away from conflict mentally while you are in the middle of it, and it's easy to get the wrong end of the stick. I just blank out sometimes and don't listen carefully enough to hear what's really happening or else run previous arguments in my mind instead of looking at what is being said *now* – and you may do the same. There is no point in having last week's quarrel over and over again. You need to listen to what is being said in the present moment before you can respond to it in a helpful and constructive way.

If you don't become conscious, you can't see what's really happening and you may miss a solution which is right in front of you. Most breakdowns in communication come from people refusing to listen to and acknowledge another's point of view or, sometimes, when they are deliberately distorting what the other person has said through not being conscious.

You do not have to agree with the other person's point of view but a great deal will be achieved in any difficult situation if you have actually heard what they said and you can offer a simple acknowledgement.

"I can see how upset you are. I understand that you are very angry and I'm sorry you feel so bad," is not giving ground, it is having the courtesy to accept that the other person has a different point of view from yours and is experiencing pain because of it. Once you have listened to them and allowed them to express what they feel, they will find it much easier to listen to your point of view.

It is even better to repeat the other person's *exact* words back to them just as they were spoken/written to you. Then they truly know that they have been heard. It is surprisingly hard to do and it is an offer of peace that is very powerful in resolving conflict.

Finally, remember that conflict promotes desire to be at peace. That is incredibly useful because it gives us the inspiration to heal the source of the conflict that keeps us from joy. And the source is always within us.

## Chapter Nine

# Health and Happiness

*"If you have not slept, or if you have slept, or if you have headache, or sciatica, or leprosy, or thunder-stroke, I beseech you, by all angels, to hold your peace and not pollute the morning."*
Ralph Waldo Emerson

Ouch! Pollute the morning indeed.

But we do – especially if we start the day by listening to the news or just with our habitual negative thoughts.

Your brain wakes up clean and clear each morning and then re-loads from the Ego consciousness. So if we knew how to think clearly we could stop it loading the negative stuff (or some of it at least). Most of the thoughts that we think are the ones we thought yesterday and the day before ... and the day and week and month and year before that.

Changing them consciously can be hard work.

It's so easy to grouch. My former colleague, BBC Radio WM presenter, Ed Doolan, says the British are a nation of "just one thing-ers."

As in: "Yes, it was a lovely evening ... but it would have been even better if the service had been any good."

"A lovely wedding; shame they couldn't keep the children under control in the church."

"Good holiday; bloody ghastly journey home of course..."

From then on, it's an easy journey into comparisons of bad service, ghastly weddings, even worse air, train or car journeys. We are so skilled in the art of complaining in all its various forms, moaning, whingeing, griping, groaning, bitching, kvetching. We enjoy moaning; it's a good way of communicating with our families for a start. And the TV and radio news is basically a load of people complaining. No matter how justified their complaints may be, they are only creating more of the same.

But have you noticed something since you began the journey to prosperity consciousness? Have you noticed that actually, a lot of this grumbling and groaning makes you feel uncomfortable? And so it should. It's in direct conflict with what you are trying to create in your life.

It's fair enough to vent anger and frustration – in fact it's important. It's the going on and on (and on) about it that's the problem.

So what has this to do with health? All sickness is dis-ease. All stress is a lack of ease. All physical disease began first in the mind, and stress is *the* major cause of disease. Much of what we experience as physical discomfort comes directly from our grumbling and moaning.

## Genes and toxic thinking

The renowned cancer surgeon Bernie Siegel, author of *Love, Medicine and Miracles* (Rider & Co) discovered that cancer ran in adoptive families just as much as blood families. He concluded that it was the thoughts and beliefs that that family contained, as well as the environment they lived in, that caused disease. Dr Bruce Lipton, author of *The Biology of Belief* (Elite Books) is now demonstrating convincingly that it is our thoughts that call forth symptoms of physical disease.

Dr Lipton is a research scientist and former medical school professor. His experiments, and those of other leading-edge scientists, have examined in detail the processes by which cells receive information. It shows that genes and DNA do not control our biology; instead DNA is controlled by signals from outside the cell, including the energetic messages emanating from our positive and negative thoughts.

Dr Lipton found that if he took diseased cells from a human

body and kept them alive in a petri dish with a suitable food source, they returned to full health. All they needed in order to recover was to be taken away from the repeating energy process of the human being they came from.

This is pretty convincing evidence that our bodies can be affected by our thinking and our environment.

When my friend Wendy was dying from cancer, she slipped and cut her forehead. And while her lower body collapsed in on itself through the fatal disease within her, her forehead healed completely. It doesn't seem to make any sense that one part of her would heal while another was dissolving into disease. But Wendy's emotional journey had created a deep resentment that was eating away at her at one level. At another level, her immune system was working perfectly.

Wendy's problem was years of obsession with the behaviour of her late husband's family who had resented her inheriting his estate. She was his second wife and the antagonism ate away at both sides.

Thoughts create things and when something rules you, eats away at you, or takes you over, then if it becomes so chronic that it will affect your health, it will show up as some kind of growth.

It has to by the Law of Attraction.

In the same way, if you retreat mentally and emotionally from something that hurts you or that you can't face, it will show up as some contraction or congestion – heart attack; high blood pressure; bowel disease.

Four months after my second husband and I broke up, I developed a large mole on my right breast which was both disfiguring and worrying. Conventional medical opinion would have been that it was potentially dangerous and should be removed. Had it been removed, it would have left a scar behind.

Instead, I took it as a barometer of my feelings of hate, pride and anger. It took nearly two years to clear all the negative emotions that had created it, but eventually, on the night after my ordination, the mole fell off, easily and naturally leaving soft perfect skin behind. It has never returned and you can see no sign of where it ever was.

What a gift that was of understanding how I would heal if I let go of the pain of the past and moved on to follow my life's path.

## Mystical and Psychological Teaching

We are all beings of pure spirit in the great collective consciousness. I love the Jewish mystical tradition that teaches that the whole of creation is happening because God/Source, whatever you want to call It, is in the process of having a baby. It, the Absolute, was so complete and in joy in itself that it desired to create another being that could experience existence for itself.

The Jewish mystical tradition says that every human soul is one cell in that, as yet unborn baby. Each one of us is on a journey of experience and seeking to find our greatest joy. Once we have perfected ourselves (realized ourselves in what makes us truly happy) then the divine baby will be born.

Each one of us is totally unique at the Soul level but we are all united at a Spiritual level as components of one great being.

For me, that explains how the Law of Attraction can draw to us the people and experiences we need to make our journey the one of perfect contrast to spark our desires. If we are all one at a higher level, our thoughts (which exist in the airy world of Spirit) will connect with other similar thoughts and vibrationally, they will draw those people or experiences to us.

We work simultaneously in four different worlds or levels: as a unified part of the great divine baby; as an individual Soul with its own path over lifetimes; as a one-off, one-lifetime person with thoughts and emotions, and as a physical body that enables us to incarnate on the Earth.

Each part of us interweaves with the others, with the Soul

(eternal) and Self (unique one-off) intertwining so much that it's often hard to tell the difference. The Self is strongly affected by what the father of psychology, Carl Jung, would call the *Super Ego* and *Super Ego Ideal* – a very basic definition of which would be the "should nots" and the "shoulds" in our lives. As in "You shouldn't be so selfish; this is bad behaviour and you should be ashamed. You should take care of your mother; this is good behaviour and you can be pleased with yourself."

The Soul and the Self are both part of the psyche – our mental and emotional blueprint, which also includes the Ego. They often struggle with how to live in order to fulfil the Soul's purpose and simultaneously be a reasonably respectable human being. When the Ego's belief system and the "shoulds" shout louder than the Soul, some form of sickness (even if it's only a cold) is nearly always the result.

This is because our physical bodies are incredibly fragile. If our Psyche is balanced, then our bodies are influenced by the upper worlds of Soul, Spirit and the Life Force itself: we can listen to our intuition and our own knowledge in order to live a healthy, happy life. In that state, we would sense when there was an earthquake pending; we would follow our intuition not to go out on a certain day or to follow a particular path in the forest. But nowadays, in an information-led world, which doesn't notice the signs and portents of the stars or the natural world around us, most often we only hear the nagging of the Ego. In addition, our bodies become addicted to substances (caffeine, alcohol, nicotine, prescription painkillers, or illegal "recreational" drugs) which help (temporarily) to drown out that data-ruled continual nagging, which can often be too much to bear. But the nagging still goes on, whether we have temporarily drowned it out or not, and as the vibrational level of our being drops and drops, we sink into sickness.

Many diseases are the Body and the Psyche calling "Time!" and begging for a rest from over-exertion; stress and an unhealthy lifestyle.

Louise Hay writes in *You Can Heal Your Life* (Hay House) that a cold represents mental confusion and a need to slow down.

So what do we do? Dose ourselves with medicines that ensure that we can continue just as we were.

It's the same with multitudes of diseases; in the allopathic (medical) system, we alleviate the symptoms with medication but do nothing to resolve the cause. Mostly we have no idea what the cause might be and, if we did, we would simply say, "But I need that job! I have to visit the family! I can't rest *now*! It's Christmas!"

Worse, if we don't do anything whatsoever to nurture and listen to our Soul, it may decide, together with our Soul Group (the part linked in Spirit) to call us home. That means dying.

## Death and Dying

Your Soul and its purpose are much bigger than this one lifetime. You are a cosmic being with a great destiny, and everything you learn goes to support the growth of the spiritual baby.

To die is not to fail; to die is to decide, "Enough of this life. Let's get to the next one!"

The Body dies and the Ego dies. If they rule our lives, we will see death as a terrible thing – maybe even evil. But if the Soul and Self are free to identify with the great One-ness of the Universe, they do not fear death. Given how most of us feel about dying just shows how out of touch with our Soul we are.

Once we die, we will re-emerge into the pure energy of our Soul and Spirit, but even though we are increasingly secular beings, we still fear what might happen after death no matter what such enlightened mentors such as the Teachings of Abraham might say. We might be judged by that old man in the sky that our Ego believes is God ... We might just be nothing.

More than that – we don't want to leave our friends and family. We have no concept (and how can we have in a science-ruled world?) that in the higher worlds there is no such thing as time and that we don't lose contact with anyone at all. The dead person is still in touch with us – the greater us that exists eternally. But here below in the Ego and Body-bound world, we do experience huge loss.

The growing industry of psychics who work to help people reconnect to loved ones who have died, shows how much we yearn for our own form of communication. But if we only knew it, we could talk to them ourselves, at a much higher level than a psychic can do on our behalf.

The main problem with physical sickness is that its invisible cause is just that – it's invisible. When we first start to realize that we create our own lives, then the natural Ego process is to start blaming ourselves and hitting self-hatred or guilt for creating a mess. We rarely give ourselves credit for all the good things we have created.

## Belief and Proof

We are trained to require physical proof that something is true but in spiritual work, this is impossible. Proof only exists in the physical world. You cannot prove anything spiritual. Buying gifts, making love or doing what your loved one has asked you to do may be seen to be proof of love – but they can only be measured in physical things such as an embrace, a gift or doing something so that someone else doesn't have to do it.

You can't *prove* love but you can *feel* it and *know* it. Your Self and your Soul recognize love wherever it is.

For the physically and scientifically-oriented, seeing is believing. But the greater truth is that believing leads to seeing.

Dis-ease is always caused by a widening of the gap between your Soul and Spirit's vibration and your Ego and Body's vibration. That creates what Jack Canfield calls "divine discontent."

When we first see or experience something that we want, the

thought of it raises our vibration with excitement or desire. At that moment, our Spiritual Self aligns perfectly with the desire – at that level there is no resistance; no Ego, and the wish is granted in a higher world. The Abraham Teachings say that your desire now exists in Universal Escrow. So everything you have ever wanted is already in some kind of spiritual waiting room poised to manifest in the physical world just as soon as the rest of you can align with that energy.

That's true for even the grumpiest and crossest people – in fact that is why they are so grumpy and cross; they are horribly out of alignment with their real dreams.

When I manifested the mole it was because the marriage break-up had set up in me such a desire for love and happiness in contrast with what I was actually feeling as my world crashed around me. There was a huge stretch between what I wanted and what I was living.

As we know, the Ego finds it hard to align with our joy and gives us dozens of reasons why we can't have it. Then, according to our ability to act consciously instead of just reacting, one of two things happen. We move towards our goal, whether physically or psychologically, which raises our vibration, or we stay where we were, feeling the discomfort of a widening gap between Soul and Body.

Enough of the latter, and we start to feel physically uncomfortable.

That's why people who are really nice, loving and giving can still get sick. They are doing so much for others that they are neglecting their own dreams. A little bit of selfishness is good in prosperity work – you have to align with yourself to be happy and then you can help others without hurting yourself.

## Tithing for health and happiness

The simplest way to return to mental, emotional and spiritual health is to return to the tithing system. But this time, do it with time and actions rather than money.

Our Martian draws to us whatever it is that we give our attention to, so if it observes us putting the needs of work, others, charity, pets, and obligations before ourselves, then it gives us more opportunities to be drawn into other people's business.

To live a healthy life, we need to live it so that we can align with our Soul. And when we do that, what is known as the "still, small voice" will speak to us, guiding us to the best ways to achieve our heart's desire. This soft voice will never shout above the Ego, it vibrates at a higher level. To hear it, we have to lift ourselves up.

So every morning, when you wake, say a few appreciations to yourself. Or, if you are comfortable with the idea, say a prayer. That's the inspirational tithe.

I use one of Florence Scovell Shinn's affirmations from *The Game of Life and How to Play It* (Simon & Schuster):

*Thy will be done this day O Lord. Today is a day of completion. I give thanks for this perfect day where miracle follows miracle and wonders never cease.*

For health, particularly, I also like *Simple Abundance* teacher Sarah Ban Breathnach's suggestion: *Blessed am I among women that I live and love in this beautiful temple.*

Next, plan or do something to celebrate your day. It's okay to plan something as long as you are sure that you will commit to it, but it's even better to do something there and then. This could be a visualization of something wonderful happening; it could be a loving kiss with your partner; it could be a drink and a biscuit in bed before you get up.

One client who has four young sons said she could never do this as they erupted at her as soon as she woke up. That summed up her life. But she learnt how to keep them outside the bedroom door while she spent that all-important three minutes of blessing and treating herself before she coped with their demands. Her way was to have one cube of chocolate to savour in bed before she got up. This is a health-conscious woman; you can imagine the opposition that her Ego and Super Ego put up to that idea (not to mention her naturopath!) But once she realized that the voices forbidding her to do something so "unhealthy" and decadent as eating a piece of chocolate in the morning were working contrary to her inner and deeper good, she went ahead and she found that it transformed her whole day.

I follow the morning tithing system twice over when I awaken. First I say my gratitudes and appreciations; then I have a cup of tea and a biscuit with my husband, and then I deal with the animals.

Next I meditate with my husband for a few minutes and then alone for longer; then I have breakfast (with a little treat) and walk the dog. Then, and only then, do I turn on my computer and check my emails.

During the day, should something happen which means I lose my equanimity, then I've learnt to stop, and do the tithing system again. Interestingly, despite all the ranting against smoking (where we use the Law of Attraction to tell smokers that what they are doing will kill them) most smokers take time out to breathe deeply at regular periods of the day. This is similar to tithing as they enjoy the treat of a cigarette (though not so much if it's a swift drag taken in desperation of course). If we were to encourage conscious smoking and stop nagging at smokers, we might find that the process was a lot less unhealthy than we thought.

If that offends you, then be aware that it has made you conscious of the Ego loading that smoking is wrong. But if you have ever smoked an Indian peace pipe then you know that cannot be wholly true. And if it cannot be wholly true then it may not be true at all. It is just data. It's when we believe the data that we make it true. Incidentally, I don't smoke but I don't have a problem with anyone who does. It's their business. And if I don't want to inhale their smoke, I can move away.

So incorporate the tithing system into your daily life in some way as soon as you can. Return again and again to appreciation, celebration *and then deal with everything and everybody else.*

For those who say, "I tithe my time," proudly, please be aware of *how* you tithe your time. If you give it to others first, you could be out of balance, even inviting ill health into your life through lack of self-care.

To tithe correctly, you would spend time in appreciation, prayer or meditation, then give yourself time to enjoy something for yourself, and then help others.

## Prayers that work

All prayers are answered; there are no exceptions. The reason why so many prayers appear not to be answered is that they are prayed at a low vibrational level of lack, and the Martian (God) has to give more of that vibration of need.

When prayers work in the way we envisage them working, it is either because they are prayers of joy or gratitude or because the person asks for what is desired and then lets go of the woe because he or she can trust that their request will be granted.

There is one other time when prayer is answered instantaneously, and that is when we are in such danger or tragedy that our Ego cannot cope any more and lets go its stranglehold on our mind. You may have experienced such a time; it's often referred to as the Wake Up Experience.

Being a bit dim, I've had to have several of those. One was as I was sitting by my first husband's bedside as he was dying in hospital. The hospital chaplain came to see me and asked me what my religion was. I said "Church of England." He then asked me my husband's faith. "He's an atheist," I said.

"Oh, I'm sorry, my dear," said the chaplain. "Jesus said, 'I am the way, the truth, the life. No one can come to the Father unless they go through me.' I'm afraid your husband can't go to heaven if he doesn't believe in the Lord Jesus."

Nowadays when I tell that story, people snort or even laugh – because my vibration around what happened is different now from what it was then. I don't believe what he said is true and it can't hurt me. But then, when I was right at the start of my spiritual search, his words destroyed part of my Ego. Thirty three years of conventional never-thought-about-it religious belief was shattered as my internal plea for his words to be untrue caused my Soul and Spirit to expand with desire. I *knew* he was wrong. I, who had never questioned a priest, and who had never had an original thought about Christianity in my life, *knew* that a religion where I got to heaven because I believed what I was told, and Henry didn't get to heaven (despite being a better man than I at that time) could not be true. My whole belief system came tumbling down.

What kept me sane (though many might not agree!) after Henry's death was my complete commitment to throwing Jesus and Christianity out of the window and finding a belief system that did not damn people to hell.

Why didn't my Ego shut me down just as it had every time before when I had heard something in the religion of my birth that I couldn't in all consciousness accept? Always before, my Ego had been stronger than my desire and it was easier to go with the crowd; it was easier not to think about it; easier not to rock the boat.

This time, however, as Henry died, I wasn't even sure that I wanted to go on living. In that kind of situation, threatened with possible extinction, the Ego becomes what it is meant to be – the servant of the Self. It supports the quest that will give you the will to live.

Since then, I have written 14 books based around my conviction that there must be a greater, happier truth and, three years ago, I was ordained into a independent sacramental church. The finding of my bliss in that long search for what I saw as truth enabled me to help others who might have had to cope with the same griefs as I had had. But I had to get myself and my prejudices sorted before I could be of any assistance to others.

## Weight and Diets

How many times have you heart a fat person say "I don't eat much; it's nothing to do with what I eat?"

They are probably right. One of my best friends eats chocolate and cake flat out and is as thin as a rake.

What the fatties among us do is think fat. Thoughts create things and you can't get slender from hating your body size and weight. And if you hate and despise yourself in a world that has a low opinion of people who are overweight then you will create fatness – and the food that creates fatness will leap to your attention.

If the world respected fat people and despised thin ones (as used to be the case in some countries where fat indicated wealth) then the odds are, you would be thin. It's what you think and believe about yourself that is the key; not the food itself. If you need a cause to hate yourself, your weight is an easy target in a world full of addictive, sugary foods.

Michael Pollan's excellent book *In Defence of Food* (Penguin) suggests that the American people's major problems with weight gain began at the same time that low-fat foods were introduced. It may be a coincidence, but it is certainly true that much of what we eat today is not actually food but what Michael calls "food science" – an arrangement of nutrients highly processed and rearranged.

That, and how we are eating these food substitutes – on the street, in the car, in front of the TV, in the movie theatre, while we surf the internet (and more and more alone rather than with others) – affects how our bodies react. Without the original make-up of food, including the fats, we don't have its automatic signalling system through our body that we have eaten enough. Instead we crave more. And without sitting down and taking time over food, we fail to notice when we are full. And, of course, the more we worry about nutrition, the less healthy we seem to become.

I've never been skinny but then, I'm not built to be a rake. However it took me many years to be at peace with that. I have been what is considered "too fat" and I've been on diets that worked. But they worked more because of my belief in them and my satisfaction at the idea of getting slimmer than because of the food I was eating or not eating. That's why diets will work to start with and become more difficult later if the issues of self-esteem are not dealt with. This is not a diet book, but what really worked for me was to ask my Body every day what it *wanted* to eat. The answer was nearly always fruit or vegetables. I can still eat my addictive biscuits and chocolate with impunity as long as I respect my Body's wishes as well.

It's vital when you want to become more slender to do it from the point of view of positivity and not from a feeling of self-hatred. From the Ego's and the Body's point of view, dieting is starvation and they will react to attempt to regain the weight and add some more in order to ensure that you do not starve to death. So a slow diet is always a more successful one in the long run (I know, I know!). Also it's unwise to refer to "losing weight" as the Ego has no concept of loss being a good thing. In absolutely everything else in our life, we want to find things that have been lost so why would weight be any different?

Instead, refer to "becoming slender" or "becoming fitter" and take interest in how you eat. If it's hard to find time to cook for yourself or to sit down and eat consciously then the problem is not within your body; it's in the part of you that doesn't feel worthy of finding time for yourself and your body.

Our desire to be beautiful, young and slender has profited the medical industry greatly through the development of surgical procedures and drugs that will have the desired outer effect. But the key to happiness is not beauty, nor youth; it is self-appreciation. Sure, have the Botox if you want; even the surgery if you want. If you do it from a point of view of moving towards your bliss, that's fine. But if you do it because you don't, ultimately, love yourself, you will have just the same problems afterwards.

Offering love to your body rather than criticism is the best start you can have towards a perfect and healthy physical life and if that means wearing a size larger jeans so you are comfortable with, then that's an Ego problem that is yearning to be healed.

# Chapter Ten

# Kick-start yourself to prosperity

Follow this simple 40 day step-by-step prosperity workout including exercises, dates with yourself, ways to change your perspective.

Feel free to re-arrange the days; the important aspect is to do something *every day* for a full six weeks in order to retrain the reticular activating system.

Be warned: this is simple but it is hard work to start with. The further in you get, the easier it should be. Don't beat up on yourself if you do miss a day but try to be disciplined. Some of the exercises can be done every single day wherever you are; others require more time and energy so sift and sort according to what your other commitments are to make sure that you do *something* from the list.

It is best to keep this work to yourself – others may find it threatening as it is so contrary to the customary mind-set of everyday life. However, if you have a friend who is also willing to try prosperity consciousness, you can gain great strength and support from talking with and monitoring each other.

## Day One
Start to acclimatize your Ego-consciousness to change by acting slightly differently in a couple of areas of your life. Wear your watch on the other wrist or clean your teeth in a different order, for example. This will help you to understand that change feels odd. The Ego will resist change because of that and changing consciously will help it to become comfortable with the idea.

Begin working out what it is that *you* truly want. Not just for everything to get better, but what is your heart's desire? Be gentle with yourself here; think of goals that give you pleasure rather than wants that bring up feelings of pain.

## Day Two

Set yourself a goal – a lovely treat of a goal – to do at the end of the six weeks. Something such as going on a visit to somewhere special; treating yourself to something yummy or spending time with a friend.

Begin to plan your financial tithing. Find or buy two pots or bags that can be set aside for inspiration and celebration and if you bank on the internet, set yourself up two savings accounts with the same names. If you have any spare cash put a tiny deposit in both bags or accounts.

## Day Three

Start to observe how many negative thoughts you have in an hour and how they make you feel. At the end of an hour, just think back over the subjects you have been considering. Be gentle with yourself; it doesn't matter if you don't get them all. But just note how you are used to the negative feelings that accompany the negative thoughts. This numbness to negative emotion is the root of all our issues. It seems quite normal that we feel bad, so we go on thinking the thought. Once you start noting how you feel moment to moment, you are beginning to harness the Law of Attraction for good.

## Day Four

Begin time-tithing. Stick a note by your bed or on the bathroom mirror with a prayer of appreciation or an inspirational affirmation.

Some of my favourites are:

*Blessed am I among men/women to live and love in this beautiful temple.*

*Thy will be done this day O Lord, this day is a day of completion. I give thanks for this perfect day where miracle follows miracle and wonders never cease.*

*Thank you for this wonderful day of miracles.*

*I align myself to my inner spirit and look for the good in all things.*

Every time you find yourself out of alignment in the day, return to this affirmation and start again.

## Day Five

Find a little celebration you can do as the second part of your time-tithing. It might be a sweet such as a fruit gum or a particular thought that you enjoy such as an image of yourself on a Caribbean island. If you are married and in love, touch and appreciate your wedding or engagement ring (and if you don't have one, get a token of that love that you can carry with you).

## Day Six

Set up an inspirational quotation to come in with your emails each morning. Many websites such as www.abraham-hicks.com or www.tut.com offer daily inspirational notes. Then make sure that you click on these *first* every morning when gathering in your emails.

If you aren't on the internet, buy a book of inspirational quotations and keep it on your desk or somewhere handy. Read one before you start work. Books such as Sarah Ban Breathnach's *Simple Abundance* (Bantam) are ideal as they have an article for each day of the year.

## Day Seven

Turn off the news. Stop watching breakfast TV or listening to breakfast radio. If you *must* listen for the traffic report switch on only for that time. Instead play an inspirational tape or listen to music. If you live with someone who insists on having the news on, either listen to your MP3 player or leave the room.

If this is a big issue in the house then it is likely that it is a quarrelsome house (cause and effect from the environment you live in) so don't push it because that will make you feel worse than watching or hearing the news; just do what you can to seek peace yourself and set forth the desire for a more peaceful home. Whatever you do, don't react to the news that you hear. Just allow it to be what it is without making it your reality.

## Day Eight
Find yourself a wonderful feel-good affirmation for prosperity. My favourites include:

*My seemingly impossible good now comes to pass; the unexpected now happens to surprise and delight me.*

*I have wonderful work in a wonderful way; I give wonderful service for wonderful pay.*

## Day Nine
Meditate. Still your mind for a minute at a time only. Practice this first thing in the morning when you wake up and any other time you remember.

## Day Ten
Fantasize. Spend two minutes a day thinking of the perfect holiday destination. Use all five senses in the visualization … use your imagination to picture how it would sound, smell, feel to the touch, imagine the flavors and all the sights of your holiday destination. If you think of a wonderful meal and find yourself salivating, you're on the right path!

## Day Eleven

Allow something... if you don't like your government, focus on letting it be what it is without protesting about it. If you dislike someone famous or wealthy, find some good in them. If you find your mother difficult, then allow her to be awkward and pushy (or whatever). She has that right. Just observe that it is your reaction to who she is that is the problem. She's always been that way; it's up to you to learn to change your reaction to that.

## Day Twelve

Make friends with your money. Take out what cash you have and examine it. Look at the pictures on each note and discover what each one represents (the internet will tell you who they are). For example, on the British five pound note there is a picture of Elizabeth Fry, who was a member of the Fry's Chocolate family. She was a Quaker and the woman who introduced the idea of education into the workhouse for women so that they could learn and better themselves. So every time you handle a five pound note, you can embrace the energy of philanthropy, education for good (... not to mention chocolate).

Doing this changes how you feel about money and that good energy will begin to circulate.

## Day Thirteen

Start gathering images and phrases to make a prosperity wheel/dream board. Look for images of your dream home; fabulous holidays; adventures; love – whatever you want in your life. The Ego needs to learn prosperity consciousness through things and the Soul wants experiences so allow yourself the fantasy of having all the things and experiences you secretly dream of.

## Day Fourteen

Start affirming the Ho'oponopono affirmation "I love you, I'm sorry, please forgive me, thank you," over and over again. Aim to say it 500 times in the first day and continue for the rest of the 40 days. After that, if you want, just say, "I love you, thank you," or swing between the two phrases. This will continue to work slowly and steadily so I would recommend that you do it for the rest of your life.

## Day Fifteen

Write the obituary that you would truly like to have at the end of the long and happy life that you dream of (and if you don't dream of it, begin dreaming!) Write about the love you gave and received; the wonderful home where you lived; the happiness that you felt and shared; the achievements that made you so proud. Go to town on this and live the fantasy. Here are some examples: (note that they don't have to be "worthy" just happy)

You are the author of a multi-million selling spiritual book that has helped the world become a happier and more prosperous place.

You travelled to every single continent in the world and had a wonderful time travelling.

You ... (fill in your own dream here)

## Day Sixteen

Remember that there is nothing more important than that you feel good. Turn off anything that refers to financial deprivation and if you do hear anything say internally and peacefully, "I create my world and that is not my truth."

Ponder your fabulous obituary and how good you feel about the life of your dreams.

## Day Seventeen

Segment your dream life into short term, medium term and long term goals. This is easier than it seems as your goals all involve financial prosperity, health and happiness. But as you already have the long term goals (you put them in your obituary) work out where you would like to be along that road in one year, five years, ten years and twenty years...

## Day Eighteen

Return to the Art of Change and put your clothes on in a different way – left leg instead of right first for example. Re-appreciate how much of a challenge it is to the Ego to do new and different things.

Review the last eighteen days and see which things have brought pleasure; which you have forgotten (a good Ego trick!) and which stressed you or made you feel bad. Drop any that made you feel bad and substitute more of what made you feel good.

## Day Nineteen

Commit to taking five minutes a day for meditation and/or visualization. Until now you've been snatching minutes here or there. This time shut the door on the rest of the world and sit alone. Either visualize some event that you would love to happen to you (as crazy as you like!) or still your mind for five minutes. If you don't do that well, don't worry

## Day Twenty

Each night from now on, think of ten things you are grateful for or appreciate each day just before you go to bed. Do this every night from now on. If you can find more than ten, well and good.

## Day Twenty One

Ask the Universe (your Martian) to set up ten good things to happen to you in the next 24 hours. For example:

I want a good night's sleep.
I want to wake up relaxed and confident
I want some wonderful, prosperous news

Please inspire me so I feel uplifted
Please ensure I am safe and all those I love are safe
I want wonderful good health/to feel much better
I want the mail to be amazing and positive
I want to be a light of joy in the world.

Not all of them will happen at once but at least one or two of them will. Then you can include those in your appreciations at the end of the day.

Repeat this two exercises night and morning and watch more and more of your requests coming to pass.

## Day Twenty Two

Set an alarm on your watch or cell phone to go off at 10am, 12 noon, 3pm and 6pm. This is to alert you to go through the mental tithing process again. Think of something inspirational, something that makes you feel good – and then get on with what you are doing again.

## Day Twenty Three

Affirm "I am who I am and I am willing to allow everyone else to be who they are." Remember this whenever anything or anyone annoys you, whether they are friend, family or in the media. What they think or do is their business and if it doesn't affect you directly, allow them to get on with it.

## Day Twenty Four

Go on a date with God. This means looking through the eyes of Source instead of your own. Go somewhere like a department store and start on the top floor looking at *everything* whether you normally would want it or not. Then allow Source to look through your eyes and regard everything as good. Say "yes" to everything you see and then move on to the next thing.

You can also do this in an art gallery or museum. You'll get some fascinating insights if you let Source comment instead of your Ego.

## Day Twenty Five
Today say the "I love you, I'm sorry, please forgive me, thank you" affirmation non-stop inside to every single person you see. Say it all day, every conscious moment. Feel yourself relax.

## Day Twenty Six
Start reading. If possible, read a chapter a day of an inspirational or joyful book. If you haven't created the time to do that yet (and you will, one day) then place a book of inspirational or happy segments in your bathroom and pick it up for a moment every time you visit.

Reading good stuff expands the mind and re-programs the Ego.

## Day Twenty Seven
Start eliminating any negative references that you may have used about money. For example:

Money can't buy you love
Where there's muck there's brass
Rich Bitch
Blood money
Money is the root of all evil
Poor little rich girl
For love nor money
Money doesn't grow on trees

Instead, remember that money is simply an energy that reflects our vibrational level. If we think money is bad it's because our vibration is low or that we either despise or envy others (which also keeps our vibration low).

Try Catherine Ponder's wonderful affirmation:

*I do not depend on persons or conditions for my prosperity. I bless persons and conditions as channels of my prosperity but God is the source of my supply. God provides His own amazing channels of supply now.*

## Day Twenty Eight

Think of ten (yes ten!) alternative ways that money could come to you. As money is energy and is drawn to you through vibration It's a great idea to open up your mind to possible avenues of prosperity. Of course there are lotteries, premium bonds and inheritances, but there are also gifts; you could find some money that clearly has no owner; you could receive a tax refund or a back-payment that you knew nothing about. You might win something. Think laterally – and enjoy!

Now return to this affirmation:

*My seemingly impossible good fortune now comes to pass. The unexpected now happens to surprise and delight me.*

## Day Twenty Nine

Today give a compliment to everyone you meet. And when people compliment you, just say thank you. Nothing else. That's a challenge in itself!

## Day Thirty

Expand your appreciation. Think of ten experiences or things that you appreciate every time you stop for a cup of tea or coffee or are waiting in a queue.

## Day Thirty One

Clear out some physical clutter. There will be at least one drawer or corner of your home that contains *stuff* that is out of date and useless. Often it is clothes; sometimes old letters; sometimes books you would no longer read. Do one drawer at a time. The emotional charge on physical clutter should not be underestimated. Take whatever is still useful to a charity shop. Burn any correspondence that upsets you (apart from tears of true love, such as a gift from your much-loved dead father). Throw away anything that is broken and that you don't immediately want to mend.

## Day Thirty Two

Clear out some emotional clutter – go through your address book and, with a pencil, mark a tick or a cross by the name of everyone in it. The tick means that thinking of them makes your heart lift and the cross means thinking of them makes your heart sink. Those who mean nothing, leave blank. Then focus on seeing or speaking more with those who make your heart lift and cut or limit your contact with anyone who makes your heart sink. If it is a family member, then just back away very gently so that you see or talk to them very slightly less. Of course if they are abusive, then you may want to move away far more – do it. Nothing is more important than you should feel good and supporting people who deliberately make you feel bad helps nobody.

Do this exercise in pencil because after six months or so, you may do it again and find that you feel differently about the people you ticked or crossed.

## Day Thirty Three

Set yourself a Sabbath day every week. If possible it can be a weekend day but if not, then a weekday is fine. Whichever it is, this a day for you and not for others. Don't take phone calls if you don't want to; don't do shopping if you do that every other day; just make it different.

If you have a family, this would be the day for eating a dish made the day before or perhaps a takeaway; just make sure that you have a rest of some kind. Working seven days a week tells the Ego that everyone else is more important than you – and they aren't. If you simply *can't* take a whole day, take half a day. Just that will make a great difference in how you feel and help to prevent you from running on empty.

### Day Thirty Four

Make your prosperity wheel/dream board. By now you should have enough images to make a collage of things that you truly want.

### Day Thirty Five

Play the money game. Work out what you would do with gifts of £1,000, £50,000, £100,000, £500,000 and £1,000,000. Remember, the exercise is to raise *your* energy not to give money away. Other people (including your family) haven't raised their energy yet so giving away all your money to them could cause them great discomfort. (this is important, people can even kill themselves with a new Porsche if they're not ready for it). Give some by all means but remember to do it in the order of tithing, even if this is an imaginary exercise.

### Day Thirty Six

Treat yourself to a cup of tea and a cake or a snack in a really smart, expensive place. When I see clients in London I always see them at the Savoy Hotel or Fortnum and Mason. We can meet over coffee and a croissant in beautiful surroundings and it costs much less than hiring an office. So instead of going to a coffee bar, go to a nice hotel. It's unlikely to cost you any more and if it does, view it as a great investment in yourself.

### Day Thirty Seven

Check out all the pictures on your walls to see if they are reflecting back to you the life that you want.

### Day Thirty Eight

Do not speak a negative word to anyone about anything. If anyone says to you "it's a lousy day" reply "It's certainly wet/cold/windy but I'm having a good day thanks." If you get a reaction, just hold the energy as part of the exercise or move away. You do not have to be drawn into someone else's reality.

## Day Thirty Nine

Write "x amount with thanks" on your cheques instead of "x amount only". If you have to write a cheque which really bothers you, draw stars and angels on it – it will still be legal tender and that will change the energy on it.

## Day Forty

Make a list of everyone you have ever hated from the day you went to school. Write on the top of each page: "I fully and freely release you to your higher good and I move on to mine."

Finally, some substitutions in case one of the day's exercises makes you feel bad:

- Give yourself a treat every day for a week, whether it's flowers, chocolate, free time or a magazine. Note the resistance.
- Change to a cash economy for a month. See how it feels to handle money rather than credit or debit cards.
- Check out the state of the inside of your car and your desk at the office, if you have one. They represent your own self-image and they are sending out messages on your behalf. Tidy and elegant? Cluttered and disorganized? Clear and clean? Dull and drab?

At the end of the 40 days you should see a distinct raise in your vibration and visible results in all areas of your life.

Now continue for the rest of your days – and watch your life transform.

Chapter Eleven

# Top tools for Manifestation

## What Works

What works is whatever makes you feel good. That's it. There is nothing more important than that you feel good. What doesn't work is when you feel a rumble of discontent, disappointment or vague unhappiness beneath all that you think or do.

Mostly we operate from the point of view of caring what other people think of us. The trouble is that behaving how they want lowers our own opinion of ourselves. And nobody's opinion of you is more important than your own.

If you don't love and approve of yourself then prosperity consciousness is a challenge.

Often we have to make decisions to do things that we don't want to do: go to supper with relatives; go to work at a job we don't like; be nice to people we dislike. The secret is to take care of your emotional journey, not constantly to be noticing what is happening in the physical world. Doing the latter will always cause you to see things which are not perfect and will affect your emotions. But if you can take care of the emotions first so that you are always – or nearly always! – feeling good, then the physical will transform to reflect that.

Make the journey fun. It is as though you are driving from New York to Key West in Florida. You wouldn't expect to get there in 24 hours and you can enjoy the journey and the anticipation on the way. If, however, you start fussing that you are not in Florida when you've got to Charlotte, North Carolina, then you can't get any further. Enjoy Charlotte; make peace with where you are. That is what moves you on towards your destination.

Once you get to the destination, your true spiritual nature will inspire you to want to make another journey anyway and you'll want to set off again. It is *all* about the journey and making the journey wonderful. If the journey is one of lack and frustration, that will also be the destination.

## What Doesn't Work

What doesn't work is expecting other people to change; wanting other people to sort out problems for you; expecting other people to do the work that will make you happier. *They* are not the power in your life; you are.

It also doesn't work if you make your own decisions wrong. Sometimes we have to do something that we don't like – from going to see your parents if they are consistently negative, to going to work when you hate your job. The answer is to make peace with the decision that you have made when you decide to do something. That makes it the *right* decision. You can then make the moves or decisions to change.

Another way to stop the prosperity process is by tuning your vibration down to the level of someone else's in order to try and help them to feel better. Doing that makes you lose connection to your own source of energy and wellbeing. Then, any help you give them is from your own energy and consequently depleting for you. It's also only temporary for them as they are tuning in to you rather than to their own connection with the Source. If you can keep your vibrational energy high, they may not be attracted to you and may seek others who aren't so bright and shining. But if they *are* attracted to you it means that they are seeing you as an inspiration in order to connect to their own Source. That's true healing.

Trying to raise your level too fast can be a way of shooting yourself in the foot. Some days we all wake up feeling a bit low. It may be biorhythms, emotions, circumstances, hormones or anything else. And if we try to be too positive then we are leaping too much up the emotional scale at one jump. That can't sustain. The answer to a bad mood is to seek any thought that brings a little relief to lift your vibration rather than something hopelessly positive that you can't handle right now.

Then just think slightly better and better thoughts until some of the cloud of misery lifts just a little. Then you can move onward.

If you are consistently unhappy with your job or your family then it's time to clean up your own vibration, not theirs. Once you're vibrating at a higher level, their negativity won't be able to get to you any more.

## Cosmic Ordering

This was made famous by Barbel Mohr's book, *The Cosmic Ordering Service* (Hampton Roads Publishing Co.) and the British TV presenter Noel Edmonds who used it to re-launch his flagging career.

There's nothing more simple than Cosmic Ordering – you ask for what you want and let the matter go. If you have no resistance nagging at you, then the Universe will give you what you want. In the case of someone like Noel Edmonds, he had already been a very successful TV entertainer so his reticular activating system didn't see any reason to resist further success.

The secret is simply not to think of the matter again. You may have experienced a passing thought about wanting to contact a particular friend and then having them email or telephone you within a few minutes. That's Cosmic Ordering.

When I was very young I thought I'd never get married and I said to myself that when I was 50 I'd have a horse (in my teens, the idea of being 50 was so very old that it would have to be past any possible thoughts of romance!) When my first husband, Henry, died, I remember saying to a friend, "Oh well, when I'm 50 I'll have a horse." When my second husband left, I said again, "Oh well, when I'm 50 I'll have a horse."

Never did I give it any more thought than that. I didn't wonder how I'd afford a horse; where I'd keep a horse; what kind of horse. I just made the throwaway remark. When I was 50 I was offered a free share in a horse. I didn't have to pay for the horse or stable her; all her owner wanted was someone to take care of her and ride her three days a week. Everything came gratis. That's Cosmic Ordering at its best.

## Affirmations

The Queen of affirmations is Louise Hay, author of *You Can Heal Your Life* (Hay House) who healed her own life with positive statements in the present tense such as "I love and approve of myself" and "I am receiving. I am receiving all the good and abundance of the Universe now."

Affirmations will work as long as a) they are positive and b) they feel comfortable to you.

Often it is easier to say "I am willing to ..." rather than "I am" as in "I am willing to be prosperous" instead of "I am prosperous."

The Ego will chatter back that you are not prosperous if you don't feel abundant. Sometimes you can out-run the Ego with an affirmation and that will work well but it entirely depends on how resistant you are. When my husband Henry died and I came across Louse Hay's work, I was at such a low ebb that my Ego didn't resist at all when I began saying, "I approve of myself." It knew that its own survival was at stake. However, as I became happier and more confident, the resistance did kick in and I found it easier to say, "I am willing to ..." for better results.

It is not an affirmation at all if you say "I am willing to let go of the fear/ hate/ anger." The Universe doesn't recognize negatives and the focus is still on the negative emotion. However, sometimes when there is a great feeling of negativity it is a good idea to connect with the fear/hatred/anger with a good shouting match or a pillow-bashing session. Sometimes you need to locate and acknowledge the feelings before they can be dissolved.

Depression is nearly always unacknowledged anger and the best way out of such despair is to access the emotions that caused it. It doesn't have to be for long, it's just about raising the vibrational level towards hope.

I'm so lost and alone; it's all hopeless.

It's not my fault; it's their fault.

I wish they would be exposed as the frauds they are.

They should suffer the way I have.

I hate them.

If it weren't for them, I'd be okay.

I know I could be okay … sometime.

Perhaps I could feel a little better if I thought about some possibilities?

Maybe I could do some affirmations?

Maybe I could just appreciate myself just as I am without judging myself?

Maybe I could approve of myself just a bit?

I'm willing to begin to get out of this.

I'm willing to approve of myself.

I'm willing to try and love myself.

I'm willing to be a little happier.

I'm willing to change and grow.

I'm willing to be happy.

## Meditation and Visualization

Meditation is stilling the mind. This stops resistance and allows the natural abundance of life to flow. It can be done by focussing on a word, on your breath or by just observing your thoughts. There are many books and CDs to help you learn to meditate and it is one of the most effective therapies there is for teaching the Ego to let go and allow the Self and Soul to thrive.

Visualization is imagining the things and events that you

would like to come to pass in your life. It's very similar to daydreaming; the only real difference being that you consciously decide what to think.

You only need two minutes of visualization a day to turn the tide towards prosperity but the key, as always, is to visualize something that makes you feel good. If you are imagining a life that you would want but feel resistance while you are doing it, the technique won't work.

An easy visualization that brings up very little resistance if you are a sun worshipper is to imagine yourself sitting on a beach on a Caribbean island (in the shade if you worry about the sun!) and use all five senses to experience your surroundings with pleasure.

- See the sea, the sky, the flowers, the trees.
- Feel the sand, the gentle warm breeze and the warm seawater.
- Smell the slight salty tang and the scent of tropical flowers.
- Hear the wind in the trees, the waves lapping the shore, the sound of birdsong, thump of a coconut falling.
- Taste a sun-warmed, ripe, exotic fruit.

## The Universal Organizer

This is the idea of using your Martian as your Personal Assistant. Every day, week or month, according to your preference, ask your cosmic helpers to carry out tasks for you. These could include:

- Arrange for the journey to the conference to be easy and swift
- Find me the perfect garage to service my car
- Help me resolve my relationship with my ex-partner
- Inspire me to find the idea for writing a book
- Remind me to seek inspiration every day
- Heal my relationship with my boss.

- Show me how to make my life abundant
- Inspire me every day

You'll notice that the requests range from the simply practical to the purely spiritual – your Universal Organizer can do both simultaneously. You can ask whenever you like or make it a formal process; perhaps each morning before you start work.

Giving the Organizer a name is a good idea (and don't worry, it will let you know pretty soon if there's another name it prefers!) That makes it more personal. It's fine to think of the Organizer as an angel rather than a Martian but just remember that it obeys your every thought rather than being able to offer you good things when you are feeling negative. Its vibration is always high so it can't reach you if you are walking away into a lower vibration.

## The Placemat Process

The Placemat Process was originally an Abraham-Hicks idea of taking a placemat at a restaurant and diner and writing what you want (and intend to do yourself) on one side of the mat and what you want the Universe to do on the other side. Then, you simply leave the placemat behind then you leave and trust the Universe to handle its side of matters.

For example:

My side:
- Go to pick up the dry cleaning
- Go shopping for groceries
- Change the bedding
- Clear my email in-tray
- Look for an inspirational website

Universe's side:
- Find me the perfect new job

- Find me the perfect affordable house
- Bring me prosperity on all levels
- Send me on a fabulous free holiday in the Caribbean
- Make me healthy

## Self-help complementary therapy

Flower remedies are very helpful in assisting you to become more prosperous. Homeopathy is excellent too but you need to find a professional practitioner to pinpoint your constitutional remedy.

Nowadays there are many different kinds of Flower Remedies to choose from, from Bush Flower Essences to Arctic Essences. I tend to stick to Dr Edward Bach's 38 Bach Flower remedies. Some of the most helpful remedies I have found for promoting prosperity consciousness are:

- Rescue Remedy – for all forms of shock, upset and also depression
- Centaury – for being downtrodden and not putting yourself first
- Crab Apple – for self loathing or low self-esteem
- Elm – for a feeling too much responsibility
- Gentian – for feelings of discouragement
- Gorse – for feelings of hopelessness
- Holly – for envy
- Impatiens – for when you are impatient for results
- Pine – for guilt
- Red Chestnut – for worrying about others too much
- Vervain – for when you feel you have to do it all yourself
- Walnut – for adapting to change
- Wild Oat – for when you don't know what you want to do with your life
- Willow – "poor me" or feelings of resentment

**How to deal with the difficult days and challenging times**
There are always challenging times in life. To love means that we will experience loss through bereavement and other ways of ending relationships. In the difficult times it is easy to beat up on yourself for feeling negative if you know that you want to be positive and harness the Law of Attraction for good.

So often we let other people's problems and issues cloud us to the extent that we get depressed or worried and we forget that it's not our job to make anybody else happy. Our life can't work if it focusses on making others happy. Other people's happiness is a by-product of creating our own happiness. That can't fail.

Pushing against anything doesn't work and neither does pushing against grief and anger. In difficult times it's important to acknowledge and experience the negative feeling in order to be able to work through it towards a resolution.

However, the principle of finding relief still works in all situations. If you can think of some things to appreciate in your life or look for some beauty, it will help to ease the pain but if you're not there yet, then find whatever relief you can to raise you out of despair or depression. At no point would it be wise for you act on any angry or envious impulses towards another person although it is often useful to write a letter to someone who has hurt you telling them what you think of them – and then burn it.

An angel letter is also very useful. This is a technique I learned from Terry Lynn Taylor, author of *Messengers of Light* (H J Kramer). This can help to dissolve hard feelings or difficult situations between you and someone else, whether they are talking to you or not and even if they are no longer alive. It is a letter from you to the other's higher self and, after expressing your views on what has happened, asks for resolution of the conflict.

## An example Angel Letter

An Angel letter to the Higher Self of ..............................
Carried in love by the Angels of God.

Dear.....
The purpose of this letter is to dissolve all unhelpful, angry and grievous links between us so that we may both move on to a greater good. I understand that both your and my Higher Selves are working for this result.

I appreciate:
*(put here details of the good experiences between you)*
I am upset about:
*(put here details of the unhappy experiences between you)*
My wish for us both is:
*(put here the outcome you would like – one which would benefit both sides of the dispute)*

The Spirit within me forgives you for any ill-will, misunderstanding, anger or hatred between us. The Spirit in you forgives me for any misunderstanding, ill-will, anger or hatred between us. You are free to be yourself; I am free to be myself. All things are cleared up between us now and forever.

Amen.

Signed......

*Now put this letter in an envelope and address it to the Higher Self of the person (or to the Angel of a particular situation, as in "To the Angel of the company that I work for"). Keep it in a special place for up to two weeks. Your intuition will tell you when it has gone. Once the letter has gone, burn it, releasing the energy to the Divine.*

## Letting your inner self in

Source energy can't follow you into your darkest places but it is always there to help you if you can just open up for that help.

The easiest way is simply to say, "I'm willing to be open to my inner self."

We can all access Source energy or our own higher self just by being quiet and listening. A very wise man once said to me that Source is always talking to us – every one of us – the problem is that we don't listen.

If you can just sit quietly and clear your mind for two whole minutes, then the Source can reach you. Then nothing feels as bad because there is hope. And from hope comes joy and peace of mind. That's the greatest prosperity – and both financial and emotional abundance will come running to you. They cannot resist Cosmic Law.

# Chapter Twelve

# Sources of Inspiration

Jerry and Esther Hicks www.abraham-hicks.com
Esther is the channel for the Teachings of Abraham a soul-group in the non-physical which teach the Law of Attraction and the Law of Allowing.

Mike Dooley www.tut.com
Mike runs Totally Unique Thoughts, a website and series of events encouraging us to open to the abundance of the Universe.

Byron Katie www.thework.com
Katie teaches the turnaround technique through testing what the Ego believes to be true. Any phrase or assumption you make, you turn it around to see the other view. For example, "My husband doesn't respect me." Turn it around to the possible: "My husband respects me." And consider the possibility: "I don't respect my husband."

Eckhart Tolle www.eckharttolle.com
Author of *The Power of Now* who teaches how to overcome the emotional bundle known as the Pain Body and live in the Now.

Z'ev ben Shimon Halevi www.kabbalahsociety.org
Jewish mystic and teacher of the Toledano Tradition of Kabbalah which helps people to understand the levels of the psyche and spirit.

Louise Hay www.louisehay.com
Author of multi-million-selling *You Can Heal Your Life* who

teaches that every thought you think creates your health and your future.

Ho'oponopono www.hooponopono.org Ancient Hawaiian teachings of seeing all external events as part of the self. Also available through Joe Vitale's book *Zero Limits*.

Joseph Campbell www.jcf.org. Mystic and teacher of the Hero's Journey to a happy life.

Steven Pressfield www.stevenpressfield.com. Author of *The War of Art* about how to overcome resistance to your bliss and your life's path.

Florence Scovel Shinn metaphysician and author of *The Game of Life and How to Play It*.

Sarah Ban Breathnach www.simpleabundance.com. A guide to becoming your authentic self.

# BOOKS

O is a symbol of the world, of oneness and unity. In different cultures it also means the "eye," symbolizing knowledge and insight. We aim to publish books that are accessible, constructive and that challenge accepted opinion, both that of academia and the "moral majority."

Our books are available in all good English language bookstores worldwide. If you don't see the book on the shelves ask the bookstore to order it for you, quoting the ISBN number and title. Alternatively you can order online (all major online retail sites carry our titles) or contact the distributor in the relevant country, listed on the copyright page.

See our website **www.o-books.net** for a full list of over 500 titles, growing by 100 a year.

And tune in to myspiritradio.com for our book review radio show, hosted by June-Elleni Laine, where you can listen to the authors discussing their books.

MySpiritRadio